The Hawke Method

PRAISE FOR *THE HAWKE METHOD* IN ACTION

"Simply put, Erik is a marketing and business god. He knows how to make a product or idea go big and has proven it with his team."

BEN PARR, *Author of Captivology and Founder of DominateFund*

"[Huberman's] knowledge and positive energy are a recipe for success in the world of e-commerce."

BENNETT SHERMAN, *Digital Ventures*

"Erik is a true visionary. The world would be a far better place if more business leaders started moving to his beat."

ANDRE BENJAMIN, *a.k.a, Andre 3000 of Outkast*

"Erik is the living embodiment of entrepreneurship. He seeks out opportunity while simultaneously empowering those around him."

ROBYN WARD, *Head of New Media Ventures at United Talent Agency*

"Huberman is a dynamic, uber-talented entrepreneur...illuminating the path to innovation, radical service, and win-win relationships."

CHRISTOPHER KAI, *Bestselling Author of Big Game Hunting*

"Erik cut a wide swath through the field of digital marketing...good things will come to those who heed his insights."

TODD JACOBS, *Partner at WME|IMG*

"Erik Huberman is an entrepreneur of the highest caliber...I expect Erik to grace the cover of *Forbes* one day."

BRENT FISCHER, *Grammy-winning Producer and Composer*

THE HAWKE METHOD

The Three Principles of Marketing That Made Over 3,000 Brands Soar

ERIK HUBERMAN

AND THE HAWKE MEDIA TEAM

NEW YORK

LONDON • NASHVILLE • MELBOURNE • VANCOUVER

The Hawke Method

The Three Principles of Marketing That Made Over 3,000 Brands Soar

Published in New York, New York, by Morgan James Publishing. Morgan James is a trademark of Morgan James, LLC. www.MorganJamesPublishing.com

Proudly distributed by Ingram Publisher Services.

Morgan James BOGO™

A **FREE** ebook edition is available for you or a friend with the purchase of this print book.

CLEARLY SIGN YOUR NAME ABOVE

Instructions to claim your free ebook edition:
1. Visit MorganJamesBOGO.com
2. Sign your name CLEARLY in the space above
3. Complete the form and submit a photo of this entire page
4. You or your friend can download the ebook to your preferred device

ISBN 9781631957017 paperback
ISBN 9781631957024 eBook
Library of Congress Control Number:
2021913930

Cover Design:
Kailyn Cox

Interior Design:
Kailyn Cox

Content Editing and Glossary:
Sam Sarkisian

Indexing:
Dani Colace

Additional Research:
Giancarlo Giron

Morgan James is a proud partner of Habitat for Humanity Peninsula and Greater Williamsburg. Partners in building since 2006.

Get involved today! Visit MorganJamesPublishing.com/giving-back

To the hardworking employees of Hawke Media,
who make amazing marketing accessible to everyone.

To the partners and supporters,
who have helped us collaborate with
so many successful brands.

And of course, to our clients,
who have trusted us with the growth of their businesses.

Thank you for making this dream of a life possible.

TABLE OF CONTENTS

05. Word-of-Mouth

06. Partnerships

07. Press Relations

15. The Future of Marketing

ACKNOWLEDGMENTS

First and foremost, I want to thank my wife, my family, and my friends for allowing this to happen. You are everything to me.

I also want to thank my co-founder and thought partner, Tony Delmercado, with whom I have traveled and worked alongside for over ten years. Thank you, Jesse Tevelow, for crafting my thoughts into something palpable and executing the launch. Thank you, Charlie Fusco, for putting the book in front of the right distributors and publishers. Thank you, David Hancock and Morgan James, for deciding to publish my work. Thank you, Keith Ferrazzi, for writing the Foreword. I also need to thank my entire team at Hawke Media for their tireless work on this project and our broader initiatives. This would not have happened without you.

There are so many people to thank that I'm sure I've forgotten someone. If you had anything to do with this project, I appreciate you more than you know. I also want to thank those who have come before me and taught me along my journey.

I'm eternally grateful.

FOREWORD

I find it fascinating how specific moments become headlines for our life stories. After working my way through the ranks at Deloitte to become their CMO, I was courted by Starwood. I accepted their offer at age thirty-two, making me the youngest CMO ever hired by a Fortune 500 brand. Good headline, right? While that moment represents an impressive inflection point in my career, it didn't make me successful. The truth is that consistent hard work over time eventually earns headlines.

When *Never Eat Alone* became a #1 *New York Times* bestseller, I knew my work was valuable to a global audience. It was one of the best feelings in the world—not because of the money or the accolades, but because I was helping people outside my inner circle. I've spent the past twenty years transforming C-suite executive teams with the concept of co-elevation, and I'm proud to say that work has been successful. *Never Eat Alone* helped me build that movement.

When we find something that works—in life or business—it's our duty to teach others, and Erik Huberman has upheld that obligation with this book. I met Erik at Summit at Sea in 2015. We were both impressed with each other then, but I'm even more impressed with him now. His company, Hawke Media, generates hundreds of millions of dollars in revenue each year. It is one of the fastest growing marketing agencies in the country at the time of this writing. And yet, he scaled his team to over 200 employees with no outside capital. How is that possible? Let me answer that question by asking another...

What comes to mind when you hear the term "marketing"? You'll probably think of related terms like advertising, billboards, social media, commercials, and sponsorships. But this is only scratching the surface. Marketing is the full experience you attach to a brand. It touches every aspect of the business, including product development, sales, customer service, public relations, and company culture.

I've watched Erik and Hawke Media help over 3,000 brands grow and succeed by unearthing the deeper aspects of marketing. He has distilled his proven framework into just three words. Before you read Erik's book, I want you to close your eyes and repeat them several times.

AWARENESS. NURTURING. TRUST.

Learn what these words mean in the context of Erik's framework, and you will go far. Whether you're an executive at a Fortune 500 company or a first-time entrepreneur, you've found a battle-tested mentor. Here's to a fruitful future, reaching elevations beyond your wildest dreams.

KEITH FERRAZZI

Founder & CEO, Ferrazzi Greenlight
Author, *Never Eat Alone*

INTRODUCTION

I want to start by thanking you for picking up this book. Though I've written tons of copy for clients and my own agency, Hawke Media, this is my first book. And let me tell you, it was a hell of a project. It's taken a lot of sweat and tears (thankfully no blood) to get this together. I am excited to share it with you!

This book should be a starting point for you to understand a general marketing framework. Take it and run with it—make it your own. Do it better. *The Hawke Method* will give you the practices to build a well-oiled marketing machine that's sustainable and formidable, one that is built to give you an overview of the strategy, but also allows you to decide how deep you want to go into the weeds.

Both Hawke Media and the Hawke Method were created under the mission of accessible, great marketing for everyone. Too many times in my career have I seen companies and individuals struggle to find great marketing help. Between snake-oil salesmen and a flood of amateurs, it is a difficult landscape to navigate. And when I have been able to find good marketers, they are generally overpriced, or want long, unreasonable contracts. All in all, they're hard to work with.

If you have ever found yourself frustrated, trying to understand both marketers and marketing, this book is for you. Marketing doesn't have to be annoying and opaque. It can be simple, it can be easy, it can be fun.

Throughout *The Hawke Method*, I pull back the curtain on what may seem like elusive marketing concepts. I'll show you how to make

The Three Principles work in synergy, guide you through my own experiences and those of thousands of brands— both successes and failures— to do it.

Marketing will always evolve, but these principles have and will not. Enjoy the moving target that is successful marketing, but leverage these general ideas to navigate it more successfully. I spent years and years honing this theory so that I could share it with you.

No matter where you are in your career—a student, a marketing manager, a CMO, a consultant, a business owner—this book is for you. It helps anyone that will or is touching a marketing aspect of business.

I'll promise you this: The Three Pillars will work for a business at any stage. How do I know? Because I have watched it work for my own company as it grew from myself to over 250 employees, and I have watched it work for thousands of clients. The nuances may change, but the principles do not.

I encourage you to treat *The Hawke Method* as your personal marketing guide, and most importantly, that you put it into action for yourself in order to get the most out of it.

Best of luck on your marketing journey and thank you again for choosing *The Hawke Method*.

ERIK HUBERMAN
Founder & CEO, Hawke Media

CHAPTER ONE

THE HAWKE METHOD

THE PROBLEM WITH HIRING A MARKETER

Marketing can feel like a black box. After I built and sold two e-commerce companies, I worked as a consultant. During that time, some of my larger clients were Red Bull, Verizon, HP, and Eddie Bauer. From the smallest startups to the biggest brands, I saw the same problem over and over again: how do you effectively and feasibly market a new product or service?

When it's time to start marketing, you have two options. You can either hire an in-house team, or you can hire an agency. It's unlikely that an individual company is going to be able to attract the best marketing talent to work in-house, so the opportunity cost of marketing becomes the biggest hurdle. If you do somehow have access to top talent, affording them can be very difficult; a good marketer makes a lot of money.

If you're able to solve the two problems of sourcing talent and paying them a boatload of cash, you now have a new problem. When you work with one marketer or a small team, you're operating in a vacuum; your marketing team only reports to management within your own company, and they're less exposed to what other industry players may be doing.

A great example of this is Pepsi. Pepsi's CMO publicly stated that they no longer needed marketing agencies because they were irrelevant (I'm paraphrasing).[1] Pepsi then released an ad created by their internal team, in which a bunch of people are protesting in New York City. Suddenly, Kendall Jenner leaves a photoshoot where she's modeling, passes through the crowd, and gives a police officer a Pepsi. Instantly, the mood changes, and everyone in the crowd starts cheering. It was an ill-inspired parody of the famous photo, "Taking a Stand in Baton Rouge."[2]

The idea here is that Pepsi makes people feel good. The problem, of course, is that you can't solve racism, war, or other social and political conflicts with a can of soda or a wealthy model, so the ad was controversial, and it enraged a lot of people. This was one of the most tone deaf, poorly conceived ads ever created at Pepsi, and it demonstrates the problems of working in-house and not seeing the forest for the trees. People do not want to dissent against their CMO, so there is less pushback within internal marketing teams. An agency, by contrast, can be more vocal without fear of forfeiting their next promotion.

Frankly, agencies simply have more spending power and better visibility on the overall market because they build partnerships with major distributors and platforms.

THE PROBLEM WITH HIRING AN AGENCY

Agencies aren't perfect either. Agencies are often built by snake-oil salesmen, who know how to sell services but don't actually know how to grow businesses. Every entrepreneur has an agency horror story, and the few agencies that are effective tend to be upmarket, making them inaccessible to smaller companies and startups. Top agencies want high minimums and long contracts, which makes them harder to work with over time. Typically, this is because clients who spend a few thousand bucks require just as much attention as clients who spend $10,000 per month.

Essentially, if you're not a Fortune 1,000 company or a super sexy startup, you won't get access to great marketing. This problem inspired the genesis of Hawke Media. I wanted to create accessibility to great marketing for everyone, and that's what we set out to do. Today, we're one of the most successful and fastest-growing marketing companies in the country, valued north of $100 million. But where did it all begin? Ojai, CA.

SELLING MY PARENTS' STUFF

I grew up in a small town in southern California called Ojai. My dad was a successful entrepreneur and he always pushed me to work hard. As a six-year-old, I decided it was time to start earning money, so I walked around my house with a big trash bag and filled it with anything I thought my parents didn't need anymore. I slung the bag over my shoulder and went door to door with my best friend, selling my parents' stuff to our neighbors. We made a few dollars and we split it between us. I remember feeling bad because it was my parents' stuff. Plus, I had to share the earnings! Thankfully, my dad was only slightly upset that his golf balls were missing.

At age eight, I wanted an electric guitar. My dad's response was, "Get a job," so I did what any eight-year-old would do, and I started selling lemonade. On my first day, I made fourteen dollars. I thought, "This is going to take way too long. It'll take ten days, at least. I do not have ten days!" (Remember, I was eight).

So, what next? Naturally, I started buying and selling Beanie Babies, which were very cool at the time. I took it really seriously and, over the course of a few months, I made $5,000 buying Beanie Babies and then reselling them at trade shows. I took that money and bought the electric guitar—and a new BMX bike. I saved the rest for a car.

By this point in my life, it was clear that I liked business, but I still wanted to be a guitarist. I remember watching *Behind The Music* with Sting.[3] He had gotten ripped off by his manager for millions of dollars. I realized that even if I was going to be a guitarist, I would need to understand the business side of things too. Then, in high school, I realized I wasn't a great guitarist. It could be a hobby, but I wasn't skilled enough to go bigtime like Sting. Back to square one.

For much of college, I dabbled in real estate, which was my father's industry, and I did some other random jobs, like selling knives for Cutco. I even started a storm drain filtering company with one of my friends. Our business was up and running by the end of the summer break between my freshman and sophomore year. I had to choose between finishing college and continuing with the business. I considered it, but I ultimately realized I didn't want to filter storm drains for the rest of my life. I was supposed to be a 50/50 partner, but I said, "Don't worry about me. Just keep it."

After college, I spent the summer studying to get my real estate license, thinking I would follow in my father's footsteps. I started my first real estate job on September 8, 2008. One week later, Lehman Brothers went bankrupt and the entire banking industry collapsed.[4] During that year, I made $350. Back to square one again.

MAKING YOUR OWN LUCK

As you can imagine, I felt discouraged when the entire economic framework of the United States collapsed just before I was about to jump in. But when your back is against the wall, new doors tend to open more easily.

Out of nowhere, the drummer in my high school band told me his dad wanted to hire me. The real estate market was crashing and burning, so I called him up. And I'm glad I made that call.

"You seem to be a bright, aspiring entrepreneur and I've been impressed watching your hustle."

He explained he wanted to harness the entrepreneurial spirit of musicians and help them focus it on making money—at least a middle-class income. By April, I had a full business plan for one-on-one business coaching for musicians, called Fame Wizard. By August, my friend's dad had raised a million dollars. I needed to go full time, so I went. I never went back to my real estate office. In fact, I left a bunch of my stuff there, and our office eventually shut down.

My friend's dad, who was now my business partner, offered me 5% of the company and minimum wage. I agreed, and, for two years, I worked from my apartment in Santa Monica helping to build the company. We coached musicians for fifty bucks a month, and we worked with 15,000 of them. We got the business to profitability, but I came to realize that it was a hamster wheel of a business. It was never going to be big.

I didn't know anything about my co-founder, who was in his sixties, except that he was my friend's dad. It turns out he was one of the co-founders of Pay Per View, on the board of Men's Wearhouse, had another company with Deepak Chopra, and more. He was super well connected. He brought in an amazing board of directors. Our chairman was Tom Silverman from Tommy Boy Records. We hired the president of Disney Records. It was successful, but as a minority equity holder, it was never going to be my big win. Time to come up with another business idea.

600 NEW CUSTOMERS, ONE DAY

Swag of the Month was a t-shirt subscription business I started with a friend in 2011. This was early in the e-commerce subscription craze. Like lots of people, I hated shopping, and we came up with this idea to send someone a shirt every month for nine bucks.

I called another college friend from the University of Arizona and said, "Hey, can you build the site for me?"

A week later, we had a one-page landing site that linked to PayPal and subscribed people for a monthly, nine-dollar shirt. We were off to the races.

I had heard that if you tell *TechCrunch* you raised money, they would write about you. I pretended to raise money, and sure enough, they wrote about it. I told them we raised $100,000 and gave them the name of one of my dad's holding companies. Right away, an article went live on the site.[5] That single article brought us about 600 paying customers on day one.

Sometimes you have to bend the rules to survive the game.

After *TechCrunch*, we got a *Thrillist* article. The author said, "The only thing better than getting a hand job is getting a t-shirt in the mail." Yes, that was actually published. The edgy article drove another couple hundred customers. Then it got picked up all over the place, including *The Wall Street Journal* and *Maxim*.

Around this time, I also realized if you write the content for a publisher, they are more likely to publish it. They want compelling, innovative content. We were lucky because subscription e-commerce was still new at the time. *The Wall Street Journal* talked about our business model, while *Elle* talked about this new dynamic in fashion. Press kicked us off. Then from there, we started putting money into digital advertising. There were no Facebook ads yet, so we were doing ads with Google and working with affiliates. After about a year, we got to the point where we had scaled considerably, but we didn't have enough money to hire a whole team of people.

My partner and I were working twenty hours a day to ship everything, market the business, and keep innovating. We were working feverishly and had no way of getting help. This is why people raise money. The unit economics were there.

We had three options: we could either raise money, sell the business, or shut it down because it wasn't sustainable. To explore the option of raising capital, I got a meeting with Howard Morgan, a gem of a person, who started a top-notch fund called First Round Capital. When I spoke with Howard, he had just invested in a company called Fab.com (which ended up being a huge disaster).[6] He said Swag of the Month was too similar to Fab.com because we both sold fashion. But he thought the idea was great and that I should keep pursuing it.

Being young and maybe a bit impatient, I figured that if one VC didn't want to invest, none of them would. Our next option was to shut down, and the universe responded. An old friend that owned a holding company for e-commerce called me out of the blue and asked if we were interested in selling. I said we were, and I gave the number that would be enough to pay my partner out and pay off all my debt from Fame Wizard and Swag of the Month.

In hindsight, I went way too low on the sale price. But at that time, I was four years into credit card debt trying to start these companies. Paying off your debt is great. But then you're broke—at least if you do it like I did. I had no job and no money, and I had to figure things out again. When I started applying for jobs, a strange thing happened. I realized I was worth more than I knew.

I got an offer to be Head of Business Development at Live Nation, Head of E-commerce at Warner Music, and a Marketing Consultant at a startup incubator called Science. Against my parents' wishes, I went with the incubator because I was so drawn to the startup life. This was 2012. The Bay Area had a well-established tech scene, but down in Los Angeles, it was still nascent. It may have seemed like a weird thing to do, but it just felt right to me. I was advising all of the portfolio companies at Science and helping with marketing because I was the one guy in the room who had sold an e-commerce business.

All of these experiences led me to build Hawke Media, a marketing agency that actually works. This book will uncover all of the secrets, tactics, and frameworks that have made us one of the fastest growing agencies in the country. You don't have to follow all of my advice.

But I'm sure of one thing: marketing matters.

ENDNOTES

1. **"(I'm paraphrasing)."**
   Hobbs, T. (2017, April 7). *Pepsi's ad failure shows the importance of diversity and market research.* Marketing Week. From https://www.marketingweek.com/pepsi-scandal-prove-lack-diversity-house-work-flawed/.

2. **"Taking a Stand in Baton Rouge."**
   Bachman, J. (2016, August 11). *Taking a stand in Baton Rouge.* Reuters. From https://widerimage.reuters.com/story/taking-a-stand-in-baton-rouge.

3. **"Behind the Music with Sting."**
   Episode aired Sep 26, 1999 https://www.imdb.com/titlett0394382/

4. **"Lehman Brothers"**
   History.com Editors. (2018, January 19). *Lehman brothers declares bankruptcy.* History.com. From https://www.history.com/this-day-in-history/lehman-brothers-collapses.

5. **"TechCrunch Article"**
   Constine, J. (2011, November 17). *Swag of the Month Raises $100k to Subscribe men to Indie Fashion.* TechCrunch. From https://techcrunch.com/2011/11/16/swag-of-the-month/.

6. **"Fab.com disaster."**
   Shontell, A. (2015, February 6). THE tech 'TITANIC': *How red-hot startup fab Raised $330 million and then went bust.* Business Insider. From https://www.businessinsider.in/the-tech-titanic-how-red-hot-startup-fab-raised-330-million-and-then-went-bust/articleshow/46148149.cms.

CHAPTER TWO

THE MARKETING TRIPOD

Imagine a tripod. On top of the tripod is your product or company. Each leg of the tripod represents a critical principle of marketing. Without any one of these three elements, the entire tripod collapses, along with whatever you are trying to promote.

The three legs of the marketing tripod are awareness, nurturing, and trust. Here's the most important takeaway of the entire book: Whenever you are analyzing your marketing strategy or a specific promotional campaign, the three legs of the marketing tripod are your checkboxes. By learning the nuances of each element, you'll be able to build a sturdy marketing tripod that will sustain your business for the long term.

AWARENESS

This is what most people think of as marketing. Awareness is how you get people to know about your product. This includes ads, special events or promotional campaigns, billboards, sponsorships, and more.

NURTURING

Nurturing is what you do between the time a person learns about your product and the time they buy your product. It also includes what you do after that. Nurturing is critical for driving conversions from leads into customers, and also for optimizing the lifetime value (LTV) of the customer. This element of marketing is typically the most misunderstood and overlooked.

TRUST

Trust is a big driver for conversions as well. A study from Edelman stated that 75% of consumers will not purchase products from a company they do not trust.[7] Trust comes from things like customer reviews, word-of-mouth, and the culture or brand you create around your business.

THE MARKETING TRIPOD IN THE WILD

When you consider the structure of a tripod, it becomes evident that without one leg, the whole thing topples over. Moreover, marketing is a competitive landscape. If you aren't optimizing your marketing, there's a high probability that your competitors will outperform you. You're always competing. You may have a differentiated product, but people have a finite amount of money to spend. It's easy to get swept up in the competition and forget about the tripod altogether, which usually ends badly.

For instance, we worked with a beauty company that saw their revenue drop seven-eighths almost overnight. Their immediate response was for us to look at their Facebook ads. My team reviewed their click through rate, the cost per click, and the cost per impression, and all the metrics on Facebook were performing just the same. Nothing had changed. We were driving the same type of traffic. Everything made sense on Facebook, and yet their revenue had plummeted.

We called a meeting.

"Hey, we think there is something wrong with your website. Have you made any changes?"

"No, nothing has changed. There is nothing wrong with the website. It's definitely Facebook."

After a week of this back and forth, we demanded to check the site.

"We need to go look at your website speed and do a site analysis. Something is wrong, and according to our data, it's not Facebook."

We pulled up their site speed. From the exact day that we saw the drop in conversion rate, their site speed had plummeted from a one-second load time on mobile to an eight-second load time. No consumer will wait eight seconds for the screen to load, click something, wait another eight seconds, and so on.

We asked again: "Did you change anything on your site?"

And sure enough, they had.

"Ah yes, we checked with the development team and they did make a quick update to the site on that date."

For over a week, they were blaming our Facebook campaigns, but they had been laser focused on the wrong element of marketing. The problem was not awareness. We were still driving the same amount of traffic to their site. It was the nurturing piece that was causing the drop. Their broken website was preventing them from converting visitors into customers. This is why you need to understand the full scope of marketing. It's common to chase down the wrong problem if you don't understand how each leg of the tripod works in unison.

The marketing tripod is the foundation of *The Hawke Method*. This isn't rocket science, and yet we see companies—large and small—falling prey to the same marketing oversights that can lead to millions of dollars in losses, or even to bankruptcy. The rest of the book will take you through each leg of the marketing tripod. We'll unpack the nuances of awareness, nurturing, and trust. By the end of it, you'll be able to take on any marketing challenge with confidence.

ENDNOTES

7. "a study from Edelman."

Ries, T. E. (2020, June 25). *Trust barometer Special Report: Brand trust in 2020.* Edelman. From https://www.edelman.com/research/brand-trust-2020.

PART 1

—

Awareness

CHAPTER THREE

FILLING THE FUNNEL

I'm in a fancy elevator going up, up, up. The executives are already in the conference room, waiting to hear my thoughts on how they should fix their growth problems. I'm groggy from the cross-country flight from Los Angeles to New York City, but it's time to perform...

WHY A NICE SUIT DOESN'T MATTER

The office was decorated as if it was Versailles; there was beautiful furniture everywhere, rare antiques, and art pieces. It was very opulent. After we walked through what looked like Queen Elizabeth's parlor, we entered a big conference room. Everyone came in and took their seats. I had two other employees with me. They probably had fifteen. Of course, the last person to arrive was the president of the company, who was dressed in a stylish suit.

This was a massive company. In fact, it was a multibillion-dollar company. They were crushing it from the outside world, but they saw their numbers falling and didn't know what to do. This was our first in-person meeting. I asked about sales and they responded that they saw sales declining but didn't know why. So I asked about email marketing.

"We're doing a ton of email marketing. We email our list all the time," they replied.

Then their advertising team chimed in, defending their efforts.

"We've doubled down on retargeting because we get the best returns through social ads and marketing on Google. We're really focused on branded keywords and targeting existing customers because, again, we're getting the best returns there."

It was like they were checking off boxes. Check, check, check. But they had neglected a massive piece of the puzzle.

Do you see the problem? After they went through their list, I paused for a moment to think. I looked at the president and the rest of the team, and said:

"So, you're doing absolutely nothing to get new customers in?"

They had nurturing and trust in the bag, but without any new awareness, their tripod toppled over.

GETTING BORED IS HUMAN NATURE

When you measure ROI directly, you're always going to get the best returns from your existing customer base. It often costs more to get a new customer than it does to retain an existing one. But there's no growth or scalability in that. If you want to grow your business, you can't keep targeting the same group of people and neglect sourcing new ones. Slowly but surely, your existing base will stop buying from you. They'll move on to something new, outgrow your product, or just get bored. No business owner likes to hear that, but it's completely normal. It's human nature. If you're not introducing new customers into your sales funnel, you're slowly dying. It's the lifeblood of the company.

This particular client had a clear problem with awareness. Awareness is what most people think of as marketing. It's the part where you're actually introducing your product or service to a new person. This was a well-organized, polished legacy company that had succeeded for a long time. And yet, they still didn't understand the need to create awareness. They were treading water without realizing it, thinking they were invincible—too big to fail.

THE REASON BIG COMPANIES STILL FAIL

At Hawke Media, we've worked with the full spectrum of businesses, from tiny startups to massive organizations, and we consistently see companies missing one or more of these marketing principles. Marketing can get overly complicated in our modern world of tech, analytics, and big data. Why was this successful, multibillion-dollar company missing an entire leg of the marketing tripod? *Excel.* Their Excel spreadsheets told them to ignore it. The data told them the best investment was in their existing customer base, and without taking a step back from their spreadsheets, they couldn't see the bigger picture.

They didn't think about the nuance of it or consider what might actually be going on with their business from a macro perspective. Despite the higher costs of acquiring new customers, you can't rely on your existing base forever. As an added benefit, if you continue to fill your funnel rather than recycling it, all the other things you've done to improve your business should increase the LTV of those new customers, which we'll get into later in this book.

> **BOTTOM LINE:** You have to constantly introduce new people to your brand to actually grow a business. This is often the most expensive part of marketing, but it's also the way to scale. When people think of marketing, they think of ads. There's a lot more to it, even within the element of awareness.
>
> For example, there's advertising, PR, word-of-mouth, events, contests, and the list goes on. Within these

areas, we can break it down even further. Should the company pursue social ads? Billboards? If it's social ads, which platform? Google, Facebook, Instagram, Twitter? If it's a billboard, what geographic location, and why?

Awareness can really be anything that draws attention to your business. The next chapter dives deep into the tools and tactics to consider when building this critical element of marketing into your strategy.

KEY TAKEAWAYS

- Awareness is the first stage of marketing, when someone becomes aware of your brand.
- Awareness can include advertising, PR, word-of-mouth, events, and more.
- If you're not introducing new customers into your sales funnel, you're slowly dying.

WANT TO LEARN MORE? Visit www.hawkemethod.com.

CHAPTER FOUR

CHOOSING THE RIGHT ADVERTISING CHANNELS

Back on the red-eye from Los Angeles to New York City for a meeting with another high-end fashion company...

They were spending a few million bucks a month on digital marketing, but they hadn't grown in a year. They hadn't really messed with Facebook or Instagram, or figured out social media yet. They were spending primarily on Google. I started looking at their Google ads more closely and saw they were bidding on their own brand, but also on very generic terms like *"dress," "high fashion," "women's fashion,"* etc.

In the next meeting, I asked the CMO, "When's the last time you googled *'dress'* and then bought a dress?"

She half-laughed. "Never."

I looked at the team of people in the room.

"Has anyone here entered the search query *'shirt'* and bought a shirt recently?"

As expected, no one had ever done that either, because that's not how people use Google.

I looked at the CMO and said frankly: "90% of your revenue is coming from searches for your specific brand, but 80% of your budget is being allocated to terms that are non-brand related, and far too general."

Marketing really isn't that complicated. If you take a step back and think about it logically, you can start to determine which tactics will work, and which ones won't, given your specific product and goals. In this situation, the client was spending a lot of money on search terms that weren't doing anything to drive revenue.

WHY YOU SHOULD CARE ABOUT ADVERTISING

This section will explain how you should be spending dollars from an advertising perspective to get the best results. You'll be able to review various advertising channels, whether it's TV, radio, Facebook, Google, YouTube, Snapchat, TikTok, etc., and discern for yourself which channels you should use. You'll also be able to judge new channels as they emerge in the future. Because it's not really about the platforms, but about how people use each platform.

You should care about advertising because it's typically the most expensive part of marketing. If you don't advertise efficiently, you can burn through cash too quickly and go belly up. But if you get it right, you can reinvest into more advertising and reach a profitable equation of money in and money out. It's a powerful way to scale.

When you leverage the appropriate advertising channels for your business correctly, you can end up competing on a higher level and become a massive company. I'll help you find your sweet spot.

FACEBOOK

A good place to start is Facebook. Most consumers use Facebook, and 99% of them are doing absolutely nothing while they are viewing their social feed. They're probably standing in line or bored at home.

This is actually a great thing for a marketer. Facebook has powerful targeting software, so you can reach the exact type of person who would have the highest propensity to buy your product.

You can do this by looking at your existing customers and matching them to like-minded people who have similar purchase behavior on Facebook. These are called look-alike audiences.

Then you can test ads iteratively, using different combinations of copy, creative, and targeting to optimize the conversion rate from click to purchase.

You can deliver this ad when the recipient is in a moment of pause, so they're more likely to click. Your audience is open to suggestions, and you're targeting the exact person who would be open to them. That's why Facebook has been so successful.

Many years ago, the challenge was reaching your demographic. The internet solved that. Every platform has your demographic. It's easy to reach people. You can target exactly who you want with exactly the message you want, on a real-time basis. The new variable that matters today is the context in which consumers are receiving your advertisement. You can target the same person on any of these platforms, but what that person is doing when they receive the ad changes the efficacy of the ad.

Facebook seems like the perfect marketing tool, right? You can reach your audience when they're ready to receive it, and you can target nearly anybody. But the Achilles' heel of Facebook is the element of timing. If you have a product or service that solves an urgent, timely problem, Facebook doesn't help you. There is no way of telling if the person needs your help right this instant.

An easy example of this is if you're a DUI attorney. There's no way to target people who currently have a DUI on Facebook. You may be able to target people in a DUI support group, but that means they already got the DUI in the past. They may not need your help anymore. You could target people who are fans of different alcohol companies, because at some point they may need your DUI services, but there's no way to intercept your ideal client at the moment they need you, which is where Google comes in.

GOOGLE

If I'm searching on Google, I'm actively looking to solve a problem. If I type "DUI attorney" into the search bar, I likely need one right away. If your product solves an urgent problem like this, Google is a good tool for you.

On the other hand, Google is not a good tool for any type of lifestyle play or impulse buy. If you're selling t-shirts and you advertise on Google, there is a very low chance that people searching the term t-shirt are looking for your specific brand and your specific t-shirt. You can bid on your specific brand name, but unless you're a ubiquitous brand or have media buzz, you won't get much out of it.

If Nike runs ads for the search term "running shoes," that can perform. If, by contrast, you're a new running shoe company and you bid on generic search terms on Google, consumers may click your ad because they're curious, but that ad costs you money, and the chances of someone actually buying your running shoes versus the Nike ones they already recognize is very low.

COMBINING FACEBOOK WITH GOOGLE ADS

Electric scooters became popular when companies like Bird started distributing them at scale across big cities. Now if I google the term electric scooter, Bird may soak up traffic there as well.

This is when your search starts to complement Facebook ads and social ads. Once you have built enough awareness, people may search for the general type of products you sell, in an effort to find you. Now you're grabbing that business too. Once you build awareness through other channels, you can compound those channels with Google, streamlining a formidable awareness funnel. But in general, Google is a place where you answer existing demand, and Facebook is a place where you create new demand.

AFFILIATE MARKETING

If you have partners who advertise and sell your product in exchange for a percentage of the sale, you're practicing affiliate marketing. It's a much lower risk than advertising, but there's less potential for reward because affiliate marketing comes with a lot of nuance and requires a robust infrastructure. When running an affiliate campaign, there's a good chance most of your time is going to be spent trying to get rid of people gaming your system, cannibalizing your traffic, or not contributing any sales.

Big media companies like BuzzFeed do a lot of affiliate marketing for brands and products. For example, if you're a candle company, you could potentially convince a company like BuzzFeed to write an article about the best candles in the world and talk about your candles. Then they would include a link in that article pointing to your site. Whenever somebody buys your candles through that link, you would owe BuzzFeed a commission on those sales.

At first glance, this seems like the best form of marketing ever. Your interests are aligned. There are no upfront costs. You only pay when you get customers. But of course, it's not that simple.

First, if BuzzFeed doesn't see the results come in quickly, they'll stop promoting your product. These affiliate relationships take a lot of effort to develop, and if your funnel isn't converting leads into buyers, you're going to burn a bunch of bridges with partners.

Second, you'll likely spend most of your time managing bad actors in the network. Affiliates may do things like target your existing customers, or promise that your candle cures cancer. They don't care about the longevity of your business. They care about getting their quick commissions and taking credit for it. They also have no incentive on the long-term viability of those customers. They may target people who make quick one-time purchases, but then the customer base churns through. You can end up with problematic or overly price-conscious customers, which could ultimately stunt your growth from a revenue perspective.

If you've built a high-performing sales funnel, developed relationships with partners over time, and you have a team to monitor the system, affiliate advertising can be powerful. If you're able to find publishers that match your business well, or you can provide a small discount on the different coupon sites, you can get a bunch of awareness without any upfront cost, and if you do your business modeling right, you can make a lot of money too.

Being choosy with your affiliate partners is important. Working with specific affiliates for specific launches can be effective, but don't simply allow anyone to sell your product whenever and wherever they want.

AMAZON

For a long time, I pushed product companies to resist marketing through Amazon because part of Amazon's business model is to cannibalize any type of traffic you would naturally get to your main site. They do this by bidding on your keywords. And guess what? People prefer to buy from Amazon versus individual companies because they're familiar with the Amazon brand and process. They're confident it's going to arrive on time, and they know the customer service experience. It's hard to compete with the biggest company in the world.

Once you put your brand on Amazon, they've got you. If you run out of inventory, they'll still market against your product and drive those people to your competitors. You've given them a right to market your products and if you want to pull out, there's no option to do that. The worst part is that you don't own the customers who buy your product on Amazon. Amazon does.

If those same customers want products in the future, Amazon is going to be retargeting them with other products, oftentimes from your competitors.

Amazon is concerned with optimizing sales across their entire site. Let's return to the example of a new running shoe company. If a customer buys your shoe on Amazon, Amazon will suggest they also buy related products like socks, but from a more established brand. They'll begin to see Nike shoes, Nike socks, Nike this, Nike that, for example. Amazon's algorithm knows the person will buy those things along with their shoes. Now your brand awareness is being dampened by another bigger brand, and you're losing a share of that customer's wallet to your competitor. It's not intentional, it's just how the Amazon machine is built—to maximize their revenue and profit—not yours.

These are all reasons why we resisted putting products on Amazon. But now, an astonishing 55% of all online purchases are made through Amazon's platform.[8] If by avoiding Amazon, you're also cutting off over half of your potential revenue, it's not worth it. We now call it a necessary evil. Amazon has become the place where people go to shop, similar to how people go to Google to search. If you want to sell your product, you should be indexed on Amazon. Amazon is a great place to advertise when people are searching for a product they need, but not necessarily a specific brand they want.

As we've seen, people don't search general terms like *"bed-sheets"* on Google to find the bedsheets they want to buy. They do that primarily on Amazon. I'm sure you've seen obscure brands appear in Amazon search results, but those brands don't need as much brand awareness because they can borrow it from Amazon. If you're the top listing for bedsheets on Amazon, you're going to sell a ton of bedsheets, regardless of your brand. If your product is typically seen as a commodity, you can crush it on Amazon. Skin care products, toothpaste, or anything that doesn't carry much brand loyalty is a good fit.

Plus, if you're creating a brand, you'll probably have a higher conversion rate on Amazon than on your own site. Being on Amazon is almost a catch-22 in a positive way. As you build your sales, you'll start to get more organic sales through Amazon. You'll start to rank higher and get more ratings. And if you can rank highly in your product's specific categories, the amount of potential revenue through Amazon is astronomical. There are multibillion-dollar companies built through just selling on Amazon. It becomes a great distribution channel for your product.

Think of Amazon as your biggest retailer. From a marketing perspective, it can build tremendous awareness and trust, but you have to figure out other ways to own that customer outside of Amazon. It will cannibalize some of your direct business. And once you're there, you're beholden to them and their rules. Proceed with caution.

PRO TIP: One way to reclaim customer ownership from Amazon is to give customers a reason to reach out to you from within your product or its packaging. You can even offer something special, like a bonus item, coupon, or an instant rebate.

These incentives and invitations will allow you to capture an email and put the customer into your own Customer Relationship Management (CRM) system.

PODCASTS

Podcasts are an interesting marketing channel because they help with trust just as much as they help with awareness. A podcaster's audience already trusts them as the host. If you do your research and determine which podcasts align with your product, it can be highly effective. You're borrowing trust from the host, who is informally endorsing or promoting your product by having you on the show, while also building awareness with a large audience.

You can't be as segmented or targeted on podcasts as you can be on Amazon, Google, Facebook, and other similar services. On a podcast, the same message will be broadcast to the entire audience, and you have to pay for that. It might be a few thousand or even tens of thousands of dollars, compared to an impression on Facebook that can cost pennies.

If you decide to do a podcast, you'd better have your messaging, your funnel, and your strategy dialed-in tight. This usually comes after you've honed a lot of your marketing strategy because you're going to hit a lot of people, but it's one hit. You're going to spend a bunch of money and it either works or it doesn't. You don't get to be iterative with podcasts. That's the downside.

The upside is the host promoting your product, which feels like an influencer endorsement, reaching a large volume of people, and advertising contextually.

For example, we found a Navy SEAL podcast talking about different tactics for survival in extreme conditions. We did a sponsorship deal with them, and our client was a survival backpack company that designed a full kit of all the survival goods you'd need in case of an earthquake or a shutdown.

So, now the podcast audience is listening to how to survive in a catastrophe and how to be more rigorous, and then the host tells them:

"Oh, by the way, if you just buy this bag, you'll be fully prepared."
It's an incredibly effective sales technique if done right.

> **PRO TIP:** Ask your customers what podcasts they en-
> joy. This is an easy way to find shows to advertise on.
> You can also search on iTunes in the podcast section.
> If you search for the name of a podcast or a host you
> like, their guests have likely been on similar podcasts.
> Search a guest's name to see all the podcasts they've
> been on. These are all podcasts that would make good
> potential targets for advertising your product.

RADIO

Radio is the old-school podcast. It's an inexpensive way to hit a wide
audience at a time when they're doing nothing. In some ways, it
reflects Facebook in that sense. The majority of people who listen to
traditional radio are in their cars commuting. They're not looking at
your product, but if you can give them enough information that they
can commit to memory, you can drive a lot of traffic (pun intended)
to your business. You also get a lot of time on radio. Most radio spots
are fifteen to thirty seconds. On Facebook, you only have a couple
seconds to get the viewer's attention.

Targeting on radio is minimal. It's broad, not detailed, so advertising through this channel makes sense when you're trying to hit a wide
audience. Let's say you're selling something for working individuals, parents, or any type of product for pets. These would all be good
candidates for radio promotion because half the country is a potential
customer. (Yes, nearly half of the country owns one or more pets).[9]

But not being able to target is also the downside of radio, so you
have to be prepared for an influx of people who may not be your ideal

customer. Even if people are interested, they could be price-sensitive, or might not trust your brand yet. You need a solid funnel and nurturing strategy to take full advantage of this influx of business.

TELEVISION

Similar to radio, you're hitting a wide audience on television and you're reaching them at a time when they're willing to receive your message. People are accustomed to commercials, and even though there's video on demand and lots of other ways to watch TV these days, there's still regular TV. In a TV ad, you get thirty seconds to talk to viewers about your product and to show visuals and audio that can really engage the viewers' senses. It's a good opportunity if you need to educate your customer or build trust.

Like radio, you will end up with a flood of people who aren't necessarily your customers. Big networks like ABC and CBS have such a wide demographic that unless you have a ubiquitous product or service, you'll see a lower conversion rate than other channels. Remember, you don't get to be iterative with radio or TV. You might be able to run a few different spots and test them, but it's not like digital advertising where you can run one hundred different combinations of copy and creative, determine which combination performs best, and optimize from there.

When we were eight months into business at Hawke Media, we decided to run TV ads. I was watching Shark Tank reruns on CNBC.

"A lot of these viewers are probably other entrepreneurs building businesses," I thought.

So we bought remnant space, which means we were buying a block of time that wasn't sold to other advertisers. It's unsold space that the networks sell for cheaper if you're not picky about exactly what show is playing when your ad is displayed. We were able to buy remnant media during the exact time they played the Shark Tank marathons. We were essentially buying cheaper ads that would still play around the show we wanted to target.

People hear about Super Bowl ad costs and expect TV ads to be insanely expensive. They aren't cheap, but they aren't exorbitant if you're smart about it. We spent $20,000 and it was worth it. Not every campaign needs to cost twenty grand though. You can do a spot for $5,000 or less in most regions. Most everyone has seen a TV ad for their local hardware store, right?

We got a massive surge from our campaign because we had solidified our sales pitch and built a piece of creative that resonated with the audience. In fact, we actually didn't do as well as we should have done because we didn't have a good follow-up method. Still, enough people needed us that we were able to profit from it. We had anticipated the audience correctly.

But then, the fickle media world threw us a curveball. The 2016 Elections started ramping up and TV advertising costs skyrocketed. Suddenly, it didn't make sense to do TV ads anymore. This is an important lesson. These are supply-and-demand platforms. When demand skyrockets, the price goes up. You've got to make hay when the sun shines and also be ready to shut it down when the opportunity passes, for whatever reason, expected or unforeseen. None of these channels are "set-it-and-forget-it" platforms. They require monitoring and maintenance.

> **PRO TIP:** Usually when you invest in an advertising channel, you want to have the budget to double down or triple down, and continue to do it. That's the essence of iteration. It's usually not worth advertising on any of these platforms if, when it works, you can't afford to continue.

YOUTUBE AND VIDEO ON DEMAND

People think that online video and video-on-demand services replicate television. Spoiler alert: they don't. Broadcasting ads on services like YouTube and Hulu is challenging because it feels like an interruption to the consumer in most situations. I don't want to see your ad; I want to see the video I picked.

If I'm watching CNBC on my television and a commercial comes on, that's fine. I was just watching the news and they want to show me a commercial. No problem. I've been trained to accept that my whole life. But if I'm trying to watch a movie or a video that my friend sent me and I have to watch a Progressive ad before I do that, I'm thinking: "I have auto insurance. I'm good. You're just annoying me. Progressive is annoying."

The companies that base their advertising efficacy on impressions seem to like these platforms, while more performance-driven companies opt for other solutions. Of course, there are nuances to all of this. There are exceptions to every rule, but the majority of companies don't see good performance on these video-on-demand platforms, including YouTube. The way I've seen YouTube leveraged well is through the content piece of it: actually creating your own YouTube channel. Influencer marketing is another approach we'll cover, but as far as advertising goes, video on demand hasn't been a great channel.

PRO TIP: Here's an edge case. Because of a law called COPPA, the Children's Online Protection Act, children under thirteen can't be targeted for advertisements online.[10] This means Facebook and Google are basically useless for targeting kids. Kids really aren't on Facebook anyway, but a lot of them are on YouTube watching shows made for children.

On YouTube, you can't target kids either, but you can put your advertisement on shows that are clearly made for children. So if you're selling toys or children's clothing, etc., YouTube is a solid channel.

TWITTER

Twitter has never been the big behemoth for advertising because people use Twitter to chat back and forth and engage with specific thought leaders. It's not like Facebook and Instagram where you're just scrolling through a news feed and looking at what everybody and anybody has to say. On Twitter, if I'm going to look at someone's tweets and you're advertising something completely different, I'm going to ignore it. I'm not just scrolling, looking for anything interesting. I'm specifically looking to be a part of a conversation.

The brands that use Twitter effectively join the conversation and engage with consumers or other brands on a content level. A good example is the argument between Old Spice and Taco Bell. The two brands staged a playful fight via their official Twitter accounts.[11]

It was a funny back and forth that spiraled into a huge discussion across Twitter. Guess what? That's free advertising.

The guy who sparked the whole thing, Nick Tran, became the Senior Director of Marketing at Samsung to help them get through their exploding phone problem, and then became the Vice President of Brand and Culture Marketing at Hulu, and then became the Head of Global Marketing at TikTok.

> **PRO TIP:** This chapter is about different advertising channels, but you can see how new platforms create new forms of marketing and advertising that weren't even a consideration before they existed. Twenty years ago, if you said a public argument between two brands could be a form of advertising, people would have scoffed at you.

SNAPCHAT

People use Snapchat to message their close friends through a combination of photos and text. The original advertising model on Snapchat was horrible. I would be snapchatting with a friend, and then suddenly a brand interjects to try and sell me something. Wait, what? Who are you? Where did this come from?

That is the customer experience Snapchat had for a long time with their advertising stories. Advertisers on Snapchat interrupt intimate conversations. Done right, it could work, but it hasn't been very lucrative yet. It's something to watch.

TIKTOK

TikTok has the highest chance of becoming a successful advertising platform like Facebook. On TikTok, you literally just swipe through random videos. There's nothing productive about it. There's nothing proactive about it. It's a great way to deal with boredom. If, in that process of swiping, you insert an advertisement that I can swipe past if I want to, it's not really annoying. And if that advertisement can grab my attention, you have the same type of experience as Facebook.

It's a *lean back*, "I'm-bored" approach versus the *lean forward* "I'm-looking-for-something" approach of Google, Amazon, etc. As TikTok gains traction, it will become a powerful tool for advertisers and marketers.

OUT-OF-HOME ADVERTISING

In recent years, almost all of the companies that have done heavy out-of-home campaigns have blown all their money and gotten close to bankruptcy. It's usually a sign that people are getting too wide open and careless with their marketing. A billboard is not a cheap piece of real estate for your brand, and its efficacy is hard to measure.

Putting up a billboard just because a certain number of vehicles drive by every day is not the way to approach this channel. You have to be generating more than just impressions. One of my favorite examples are the billboards about Academy Award nominated movies that pop up all over Los Angeles during Oscar season. The movies' marketing teams do this because they want to get votes, and LA is a targeted region for voters at the Academy who will likely see the billboards.

We have also talked about buying the billboard near our office so that when people are driving to our building for a meeting, they see a billboard with our logo on it. Now we have more credibility.

You've probably seen the billboards for food chains like McDonald's on the highway. Every fast food chain does this and it makes total sense. People on long drives see a big sign for McDonald's. That's compelling because it's not just an impression, it's a way to bring hungry people to their location, which presumably can't be seen directly from the highway.

In these examples, it's not about impressions or general awareness. There's an ulterior motive. Generally, we have not seen a lot of efficacy for out-of-home ads except for in these types of strategic scenarios. There are a lot of interesting technologies being developed in this area, though, so it feels ripe for innovation and improvement.

NATIVE ADVERTISING

Our partner, Taboola, is an expert in native.[12] They think this form of advertising is not only a powerful channel, but the single most powerful channel of all. Native advertising is any ad that fits the form, feel, and function of the media in which it appears. It helps marketers to place camouflaged ads that are so cohesive with the page content, assimilated into the design, and consistent with the platform behavior that the viewer feels the ad belongs there.

Counterintuitively, Taboola suggests making the creative stand out from the other content surrounding it by having a clear, singular point of focus and using a distinct, eye-catching image or video, while remaining within the audience's expectations of the form. Headlines should be honest but exciting. Remember, the post-click experience matters too, so make sure the copy is relevant to your ad. And be sure to test your creative on native platforms deliberately and consistently (every two-to-four weeks). Don't test too much at a time, either. Stick to five-to-twelve variations of titles and images.

Native is a powerful addition to your media mix. If you're just starting out, the best solution is to work alongside other channels that are already working for you, and accurately attribute the impact on your whole funnel. Selecting native advertising as a channel will give your brand the ability to borrow the authority of the surrounding content, as well as to meet new consumers when they're open to discovering something new. Taboola calls this, "the moment of next."[13]

KEY TAKEAWAYS

- Advertising is typically the most expensive part of marketing.
- If you don't advertise efficiently, you can burn through cash too quickly. But if you get it right, you can reinvest into more advertising and reach a profitable equation. It's a powerful way to scale.
- When you're developing your advertising strategy, it's important to understand how to measure various channels, and also how to take advantage of each one based on how consumers interact with them.
- Don't generalize the demographics for any of these channels. For example, "No Gen Z is on Facebook." Most Gen Zs probably are not on Facebook, but Facebook has billions of people. There are still a bunch of Gen Zs on Facebook who you can reach. These are all the things you have to explore when determining which channel to use and how to use it. It's never black and white.

WANT TO LEARN MORE? Visit www.hawkemethod.com.

ENDNOTES

8. "55% of all online purchases."
Rey, J. D. (2016, September 27). *55 percent of online shoppers start their product searches on Amazon.* Vox. From https:// www.vox.com/2016/9/27/13078526/amazon-online-shopping-product-search-engine.

9. "nearly half of the country."
US pet population and ownership TRENDS 2019-2020: Dogs, cats and other pets - ResearchAndMarkets.com. Business Wire. (2020, July 20). From https://www.businesswire.com/ news/home/20200720005393/en/US-Pet-Population-and-Ownership-Trends-2019-2020-Dogs-Cats-and-Other-Pets---ResearchAndMarkets.com.

10. "COPPA."
16 CFR Part 312 -- Children's online privacy Protection Rule. 16 CFR Part 312 -- Children's Online Privacy Protection Rule. (1998, October 21). From https://www.ecfr.gov/current/title-16/ part-312.

11. "Old Spice and Taco Bell."
Old Spice Twitter Account @OldSpice. (2012, July 9). *Why is it that "fire sauce" isn't made with any real fire? Seems like false advertising.* Twitter. From https://twitter.com/OldSpice/ status/222410960051240960.

12. "Taboola."
Sourced directly from interview with Hawke Media Partner, Taboola, 2021. For more information on Taboola, see https:// www.taboola.com/.

13. "the moment of next."
Nielson, & Taboola. (n.d.). *Nielsen and TABOOLA Define moments of next.* Nielsen and Taboola Define Moments of Next. From https://go.taboola.com/nielsen-whitepaper/.

CHAPTER FIVE

WORD-OF-MOUTH

Hawke Media is a bootstrapped company. We didn't raise money, so we had limited cash in the early days, and we certainly didn't have any budget for ad campaigns. I spent a lot of my time meeting individual people and explaining our value proposition, but I couldn't keep that up forever. There was no scalability in it. I pondered the best way to get the word out, and decided we needed a short, differentiated tagline to help people talk about us.

I tried different things, like, "We're a digital agency." But everyone hates digital agencies. They have a bad connotation.

I tried: "We're a marketing agency."

Same result. I couldn't play into the same old terms. *How could I describe us?*

For most of our early clients, I wasn't just a consultant, I was serving as their Chief Marketing Officer. So I started using that specific term, calling Hawke Media "Your Outsourced CMO." When I said that, people went from turned off to turned on. Their eyes lit up with the idea of an outsourced CMO.

"Finally, an expert who can solve my marketing problems!"

Through simple trial and error, I was able to test the market and read people's reactions. "Your Outsourced CMO" was clearly the best tagline, so I started telling *everyone*. And it worked. My phone started ringing and I started getting emails.

Sometimes it would be an introduction from a friend saying, "Hey, this is Erik. He's like your outsourced CMO. You should talk to him about your marketing."

Sometimes, random people would just reach out and say, "I heard you're an outsourced CMO. I really need that right now."

I had stumbled upon a simple way to articulate our offering, using language that resonated with our target market. By doing this, we differentiated ourselves and avoided the negative connotations that come with being an agency. The most important part of all this, though, is that we gave *other* people a way to articulate what we do.

Without our tagline, it can be hard to describe us.

"They're a marketing team, but they work with you as consultants. But it's completely outsourced. So it's a digital agency, but more involved."

That's just awkward and makes everyone uncomfortable. But with our refined tagline, anyone who knows about us or learns about us subconsciously feels like they can be one of our sales reps, *and they want to sell our product.*

It's amazing what a few specific words in the correct sequence can do for your marketing.

THE #1 DRIVER TO SUCCESS IN YOUR BUSINESS

In this section, we'll explore how to optimize word-of-mouth for your business. Word-of-mouth is the #1 driver to success. Without it, you would need to buy every customer with ads, which isn't scalable. You need your own customers, your community, and people in general to be your best sales team. This is critical for any company. If you succeed in driving word-of-mouth marketing, you'll notice it has a viral effect, acting as a force multiplier on all of your other marketing efforts. As a quick example, imagine that you and your top competitor both run ads to acquire customers. You both have the same ad spend, but your competitor is able to convince their customers to refer a friend through word-of-mouth. For every customer you acquire, your competitor acquires two. Here's another way to put it: Just by having effective word-of-mouth, the competitor will grow twice as fast, with the same ad spend.

This viral growth element is called a K-Factor or Viral Coefficient, which is basically the word-of-mouth multiplier on all of your other marketing efforts.

THE DRIVE-BY PITCH

An elevator pitch works when you are actually stuck in the elevator with your potential customer. But how often does that happen? From a scalability perspective, you'll never grow if you have to make an elevator pitch to every customer you acquire. An elevator pitch is great if you have a bit more time with a prospect, and you should definitely have one if you're building a sales team. But still, from a lead-generation standpoint, it's hard to get people in the door at scale if that's your only option. You need something faster but just as effective.

We call our shortened pitch the "drive-by pitch." The drive-by pitch distills the elevator pitch down to five-to-seven words (or shorter—three words in the case of Hawke Media). It should be short enough to say into a megaphone as you drive past your ideal customer on the highway—although we don't recommend doing that.

It answers questions like: Who are you? What do you do? What are you about? Why should I be interested?

The purpose of the drive-by pitch is to hook people into a deeper discussion later, and to empower them to re-pitch others in the process. It's not about closing the deal, or even explaining what you do in detail. It's about communicating your unique value in an instant.

To be clear, this is not always necessarily your company's outward-facing tagline like it is for Hawke Media. People don't describe Nike by saying "Just Do It." The drive-by pitch is an explanation that can be easily inserted into other people's conversations. What is your one sentence that will shift your word-of-mouth marketing machine into high gear?

GUIDELINES FOR CREATING YOUR OWN DRIVE-BY PITCH

Every company should have a drive-by pitch. Here are some guidelines for creating your own.

1. MAKE IT SUPER SIMPLE.

If people like your product or service and it's easy to describe, they'll mention it to others.

2. COMMUNICATE THE VALUE PROPOSITION.

If your value proposition is clear, people will feel they are providing value to their friends, as opposed to selling something to their friends. With a good drive-by pitch, you've also made it really simple for them, so it's not uncomfortable.

3. TEST DIFFERENT VARIATIONS.

See whether people get excited or not. When it's early, the

founder is always the main salesperson. You need to have some emotional intelligence throughout this process to read people's reactions. You have to be honest and ask yourself: "Is it resonating, or not? Are people genuinely interested, or are they just giving me a pat on the back because they want to be supportive?" Don't give a long-winded explanation. Five-to-seven words. Pause. Gauge the reaction. Repeat until something sticks.

Hawke Media is *Your Outsourced CMO®*. Why does this drive-by pitch work for us? It's deeper than you might think. These three words communicate quite a lot about our business and brand.

1. EXPERIENCE AND QUALIFICATIONS.
Immediately, we have a higher level of efficacy and experience than most competitors because we are not just marketers, we are your CMO.

2. SIMPLICITY AND EASE OF USE.
Marketing is a hard task. Finding the right hire to fill the CMO role can be a headache. What if you could just outsource it, and get the same or better results?

3. QUALITY, PROFESSIONALISM, CONCIERGE SERVICE.
A CMO is a C-Suite position. This connotes a certain level of experience and know how. "Your" and "Outsourced" are also both service-oriented terms.

4. WHAT WE DO.
A CMO is in charge of the entire marketing department. From this, you can infer that we're able to fulfill all of those tasks.

5. HOW WE DO IT.
If we're an outsourced CMO, we presumably act in that capacity for various clients, on some sort of contract or monthly rate.

As you can see, our three-word, drive-by pitch communicates our value from multiple angles, and it attracts our ideal customers: companies that need a high-level marketer to take over their strategy and execution. All the fat has been trimmed from the message.

You see, we didn't use a complicated, machine-learning algorithm or qualitative, feedback surveys to create our pitch. I went out and talked to people. I talked to my potential customers, watched the reactions, saw when it resonated, and doubled down.

DON'T BE THE Y OF X

Avoid analogies like, "We are the Uber for X." You shouldn't associate yourself with another brand. It can have an adverse effect. If I say we're the Uber for car washes, some people might think we're bullies, because Uber's brand has become synonymous with bullying.[14] People might ask, "Do you just let anyone wash my car? Because Uber doesn't seem to have any qualifications for their drivers."

You can see how this is a slippery slope. When you associate your business with another brand, you might get the positive associations, but all the negatives, too. Worse, you seem less innovative. So instead of the "Uber for car washes," you could say, "We're on-demand car washes. Order your wash and we'll come to your house, same day, and get the job done, hassle free."

If you want to take it a step further, find your own language for "on-demand." This makes it more unique. For example, "Car washes that come to you." Cool. Your language choices matter. Now when someone says, "Ugh, my car is filthy," you can say, "Oh, you should check out this company, they do car washes that come to you."

Bingo.

TO INCENTIVIZE OR NOT TO INCENTIVIZE

Tom Silverman is a legend in the music business. He discovered Queen Latifah, Naughty by Nature, Method Man, and other household names in the world of Hip Hop.[15] He was on our board of advisors at my musician-business-coaching company, Fame Wizard, and I remember him speaking to a big group of artists about the idea of paying fans to bring other fans to their concerts. Fans could be paid a few dollars per referral, for example, depending on the ticket price. Tom felt this was *not* a good idea, which piqued my interest.

Since then, I have seen this in action, and Tom was right. If I like something, I instinctively want to share it because I want to bring other people the same value I am receiving. But if you incentivize it, and if that incentive is not meaningful, it will diminish the value and you could actually counteract my inclination to share.

For example, if I really like your book, I am going to tell all my friends, "Hey, this book is great. I learned so much from it. You should read it." And that's enough for me. I feel good about that because I just created value.

But if you then tell me, "Erik, I will give you ten cents for every book you sell for me," I am not going to do anything because ten cents means nothing to me. And now I have to worry about selling your book. It's become a dreaded task. Instead, I am going to opt out and not participate at all. By offering an incentive that does not fit the effort, you can actually hurt word-of-mouth.

To counter that point, we've seen massive success in companies like Uber, LinkedIn, and Dropbox with their referral programs.[16] DropBox had one of the most successful referral programs of all time, in which they gave people extra space for referring their friends, and that worked.[17]

League of Legends by Riot Games offered another great incentive program.[18] When they initially launched League of Legends, Riot knew they had a loyal, hardcore gamer audience who loved the game, so they created a tiered system for referrals. For one referral you get prize X, for five referrals you get prize Y, and for twenty referrals you get prize Z. They even had a tier for if you referred 1,000 people. 1,000! If you reached that tier, they would fly you to LA and create a character in the game based on you. I don't know that anyone ever hit that number, but they created that path, and people actually competed to see how high they could get.

Tesla offers some referral prizes as well.[19] Refer one person and get a free charge, refer five people and get a t-shirt, etc. This is almost comical, and Elon Musk knows that. The idea here is that the community of people buying a Tesla is small, so existing owners are likely to know other potential customers. I referred four or five people to Tesla and got them to buy cars. I loved mine, and it made me feel special and cool to refer friends. In the case of Tesla, there was value in actually referring people because it made you feel included within an elite club.

> **PRO TIP:** When you're considering incentives for word-of-mouth referrals, get creative. Monetary referral rewards can sometimes fall flat. More custom or unique rewards can work well in the right context.

HOW TO SELL WITHOUT SELLING

Red Bull is one of the most interesting companies from a marketing perspective because they have a fantastic product, an energy drink, and yet 99% of their marketing has nothing to do with selling it. They don't talk about energy drinks. Early on, they had commercials with the tagline, "Red Bull gives you wings," but they were never pushing the message, "You Should Drink Red Bull."

Instead, they identified their audience and asked, "Why does someone buy a Red Bull?" Someone buys a Red Bull because they want energy. People who want energy are probably interested in extreme sports, danger, and adventure; they most likely enjoy things like mountain biking, snowboarding, surfing, stunts, and events like the Red Bull Flugtag and the Red Bull Air Race.

Red Bull has invested billions of dollars into its media house that publishes content featuring extreme sports and dangerous stunts. Remarkably, it not only fueled one of the most successful beverage companies in history, but it has also become a profitable and successful media house in its own right. Do you remember where you were when the Red Bull Space Dive aired? I'm betting you at least remember hearing about it. That's the power of knowing your audience and giving them word-of-mouth marketing opportunities.

Red Bull isn't going to share their Amazon product page on social media, and neither will you. No one is going to send a link to their friends to buy Red Bull on Amazon. That is just not what people do. But the number of social shares generated from an astronaut jumping out of space with the Red Bull logo everywhere was astronomical (pun intended).[20]

The people who gravitate toward that kind of an event tend to want more energy. Red Bull is basically saying, "We can give you the energy to jump out of space. You want to do it, too? Go drink a Red Bull."

Red Bull's promotions suggest that these adrenaline-soaked events are a natural pairing for their brand. That marketing works for a few reasons. First, it engages your audience above and beyond a simple purchase decision. Second, it gives them something to share that isn't pushing your product, but *is* pushing your brand. It thereby allows the person sharing to feel like they're creating value. They are sharing content that they think their friends and family will enjoy. Naturally, if the content is aligned with your product, you will drive more sales. And you will also increase word-of-mouth.

> **PRO TIP:** Time-sensitive campaigns are useful in driving word-of-mouth. For example, you could run a sale: "This month, for every product we sell, we are going to donate 10% to charity X." That gives people urgency, and something to talk about beyond the product itself.

In relation to your marketing funnel, word-of-mouth sits outside of it, but also flows through it. It's everywhere. If I am already aware of your company or brand and then someone tells me you're great, it's just more reinforcement. This plays into trust, which we'll discuss later in the book.

KEY TAKEAWAYS

- Word-of-mouth is not just an option or a bonus. It's a must-have.
- Having a great product or service will always be the #1 driver for word-of-mouth marketing.
- Without word-of-mouth, you would need to buy every customer with ads, which isn't scalable.
- If you succeed in driving word-of-mouth marketing, it has a viral effect, acting as a force multiplier on your other marketing efforts.
- The K-Factor or Viral Coefficient is the word-of-mouth multiplier on your other marketing efforts.

WANT TO LEARN MORE? Visit www.hawkemethod.com.

ENDNOTES

14. "Uber's brand has become."
Siddiqui, F., & Albergotti, R. (2020, October 22). *Uber drivers sue app over 'constant barrage' PUSHING CALIFORNIA anti-employment initiative.* The Washington Post. From https://www. washingtonpost.com/technology/2020/10/22/uber-prop22-suit/.

15. For more information on Tom Silverman and his company, Tommy Boy Music, see:
https://www.tommyboy.com/

16. "Uber, LinkedIn, and Dropbox Referral Programs"
Dropbox: https://help.dropbox.com/accounts-billing/space-storage/earn-space-referring-friends. Uber: https://www. uber.com/legal/nl/document/?name=referral-program-rules&country=united-states&lang=en. Linkedin: https://www. linkedin.com/business/talent/blog/product-tips/how-linkedin-is-using-linkedin-referrals.

17. "most successful referral programs of all time"
Veerasamy, V. (2014, January 21). Here's how dropbox copied its referral program from paypal. Referral Candy. From https:// www.referralcandy.com/blog/dropbox-referral-program/.

18. "League of Legends."
The referral program referenced has since been phased out. Learn more about the game here: https://www.leagueoflegends.com/.

19. "Tesla Referral Program."
For more information see: https://www.tesla.com/support/ referral-program.

20. "social shares generated."
Bedi, A. S. (2015, June 15). *Red Bull- STRATOS Campaign.* SlideShare. From https://www.slideshare.net/amrit1991bedi/ red-bull-stratos-campaign-49393645.

CHAPTER SIX

PARTNERSHIPS

"Have you met Ted?"

Let me take a step back. Ted isn't actually my friend. He's a character in the popular television show *How I Met Your Mother*. In the show, whenever Ted and his friend Barney are hanging out at the bar, Barney approaches an attractive girl and asks:

"Haaa-ve you met Ted?"

I refer to this line with my team at Hawke Media on a regular basis. Barney doesn't know the girl at all, but Ted is a single guy and Barney wants to hook them up. This is Barney's way of creating third-party validation prior to Ted's interaction. It immediately gives him street credit from a friend—someone who presumably knows Ted well.

This same method works in marketing.

Even if the prospect doesn't know the partner well, or even if there's a low level of trust, warm introductions work better than cold ones. But partners can do a lot more than make introductions.

In this chapter, we'll go through the biggest benefits of using partnerships as the foundation of your marketing strategy.

THRIVING DURING BLACK SWAN EVENTS

When COVID-19 went global in early 2020, we were expecting it. We had been watching it for a couple of weeks, wondering if we would have to wait for quarantine or send our people home, similar to what China had already done. Then, on March 13, I got a call from a well-connected friend who told me the president was about to declare a national emergency. After the call, I sent everybody in the office home.

"Go home and sit tight. We don't really know where this is going."

That weekend was one of the most stressful weekends of my life because I didn't know if I would be going back in on Monday or if my entire business would be gone. I felt helpless until I realized I could get more visibility from our partner network. I began to share internal information with certain partners, and they shared back.

"Here is what we are seeing. This is what's happening on our end."

We were able to see which industries were declining and which industries were growing, nearly in real-time, and not just from our own anecdotal data, but also from partners with massive customer bases. We knew home buying was up, but luxury goods were taking a little bit of a hit, so we could communicate these trends with our customers and help them navigate the rapidly changing environment.

We could confidently tell certain customers: "If you pull back your marketing now, all of your competitors will succeed around you." Or, "Your industry is hurting, so consider reducing ad spend in the short term. Your customer base is price conscious on this type of purchase right now."

We were able to retain a lot of business this way, and we were doing right by our clients because we had data. It was not a guess. Some companies became wildly successful through the pandemic because we had these insights. Our partner network helped in two ways. First, it provided us with data and knowledge that allowed us to inform our clients and make good decisions. We were able to share information with a pool of people that allowed us to not only calm down a little bit (because we actually had the information we needed), but also allowed us to share which customers were doubling down, which customers we should be pulling back on, which industries were affected, and more. We were able to strategize effectively because we were analyzing it as a group versus only considering our individual ecosystems.

Second, we were directly referring business to each other and looking out on account of mutual interests. One of our best months for outbound and inbound leads was June 2020, right after the pandemic had exploded in the United States. It scaled from March to June, so it was a huge growth period in that part of the business for us. When things are tough, people look to their community. Partnerships got us through what could have been the end of our company because we supported each other, referred business to each other, and shared our knowledge collectively.

EXPONENTIAL PARTNERSHIP MATH

In a good partner relationship, one plus one equals four. If you are bringing your clients to a partner and they are bringing their clients to you, it multiplies both sides. That's how we look at it.

Partners amplify awareness and trust. If someone comes to your business through a Facebook ad and you tell them your product is awesome, they might think, "Why should I trust you? You showed me an ad. You're just trying to sell me."

On the other hand, if another company says your product is awesome, it establishes third-party validation. Because of this validation, the conversion rate on a partnership-driven lead is going to be a lot higher than your standard lead. You'll also get a higher average-order value and lifetime value because the audiences are aligned. Timing is not going to be an issue for these customers either. The partner is introducing you, so the prospect needs you now.

GROWING WITHOUT SPENDING

More often than not, partnerships do not have a direct cost. If you align with a partner and they see an equal value in cross promotion, you don't have to outlay any cash. It's a great way to scale. A lot of companies constantly dump money into advertising to drive growth, but with partnerships, you can get the same or better results without spending a dime.

In a healthy partnership, both parties bring equal value. The biggest brands in the world are not going to partner with a tiny start-up unless there is some PR value or something else in the deal. Otherwise, it isn't an equal exchange of value and the parties become misaligned. As you grow, you can continue finding new partners at your current size and increase the quality of your partners. This can be time consuming, but it is a great way to scale without having to spend hard cash.

Speaking of partners and third-party validation, my team and I made a dedicated effort to include their quotes and ideas within this book. This next one is from GQ Fu, the Founder and CEO of LTVplus:

> *"Having great partnerships with agencies and technology partners has been crucial to [our] growth. Creating and nurturing these partner relationships through value creation and co-marketing helps both parties scale together at the same time."*[21]

HOW TO GET PARTNERS

Potential partners are all around you. Finding them is relatively easy. (**SPOILER ALERT:** Sending automated response messages on LinkedIn is not the right approach.) When you acquire some initial customers, ask them what else they like. If your business is B2B (business-to-business), ask them which other companies are supporting them. If you're a B2C company (business-to-consumer), ask your customers what other products they're buying. What other shops do they like? Just finding that alignment alone allows you to reach out to these targets and open the conversation.

"Hi, I have been talking to our customers and noticed that they buy a lot of your products as well as ours. We should talk about a partnership."

Remember, the value is mutual, so you're immediately offering value, assuming you have an audience for them to reach. And they are more likely to be interested because you took the time to do that research and confirm a good fit.

For B2B companies, you can always ask, "Who else services you?"

For example, we're a marketing company, so we can ask our clients, "Who do you use for your accounting?" Now, we can go talk to those accounting companies, tell them we have some crossover in customers, and open up the same partner discussion.

You can also build partnerships with value-added retailers. With this approach, you would work with a bigger company to bake your product into their offering as an upsell. GoDaddy is notorious for doing this. Once you register a domain, they offer all kinds of value-added services and tools. But these tools aren't built internally at GoDaddy. They're built by other partners, selling through GoDaddy's funnel and giving GoDaddy a percentage of sales.

In the software business, automated cross selling is common. On the manual side, if you have a sales team, you can match them up with other sales teams selling the same customer other products, and then find ways to refer business. For example, we could partner with an email software company. We can tell our customers that we recommend our partner's email software, and the partner can tell their customers they recommend us as a good agency. It creates a constant, mutually beneficial back and forth.

Another example of this is a collaborative marketing strategy called cross-store selling. This is when two or more DTC (direct-to-consumer) brands partner together to sell or supply each other's products without a traditional wholesaling relationship. For example, you might run an online retail store selling bicycles but may not be selling helmets and other accessories. To expand your product catalogue with the additional items would typically cost you a great deal of time, money, and resources. Instead, you could partner with another store that sells helmets and seamlessly add their products to your site with no upfront costs or inventory commitments. Cross-store selling enables merchants to drive brand awareness, acquire new customers, and increase their LTV and AOV (average-order value) by leveraging their brand partner's website traffic and complementary products.

> **PRO TIP:** The most effective way to take advantage of this strategy is by joining a cross-store sales network such as Carro. The Carro network includes tens of thousands of DTC brands, and syncs inventory management, sales transactions, and fulfillment between partners in real-time.

Cross promotion and combined content can also be highly effective. This includes launching content initiatives together, like doing a joint webinar or co-producing content. An example would be GoPro filming a Red Bull campaign that markets both brands, and then both companies promoting the campaign. They are building each other's brands simultaneously. You see it all the time with retailers. Another example is iPhones being sold by AT&T. Apple and AT&T produce commercials together as partners, and they both benefit, so their dollars go further.

CREATE A LASTING BUSINESS

At Hawke Media, we now have hundreds of partner companies looking out for us every day. And we look out for them. We have systematized it, a gift that keeps on giving. We were named one of the fastest-growing marketing companies in the country by Inc., and most of our business is generated through partnerships.[22] Whether Facebook changes its algorithm, or a global pandemic strikes, those partnerships will hold strong. The only way to kill a partnership is to be a bad actor or to screw over your partner.

Don't do that. Otherwise, assuming you keep your value proposition, your partners will keep helping you.

We generate leads, pass information around, and do deals with our partners on a regular basis. Eventually, this develops into an ecosystem. It becomes a moat you've built around your business. When the market falls and things get tough, you'll weather the storm together. If someone gives you a bad review, your partners will chime in.

"I've worked with them on a bunch of business. It sounds like you had a bad experience, but in general, they're great."

Partners can be your ear on the street, which we have seen a lot. One previous client might be badmouthing us, but because we have an army of partners in our corner, they can shut it down. Every company, at some stage, is going to have angry customers. It comes with the territory.

To recap, well-aligned partnerships will drive the best possible customers to your business. You'll see a higher conversion rate and a higher lifetime value. Partnerships drive awareness and trust, and there is often no upfront cost or dollars exchanged. It's all about long-term success. Relationships are far more robust than a platform, or a software, or a tactic. If you can build strong relationships with partners and make it the foundation of your business, you've built a bulletproof system for sustained growth.

KEY TAKEAWAYS

- Partners can endorse your product to establish third-party validation.
- More often than not, partnerships do not have a direct cost.
- In a healthy partnership, both parties bring equal value.
- You can build partnerships with bigger companies to bake your product into their offering as an upsell.

WANT TO LEARN MORE? Visit www.hawkemethod.com.

ENDNOTES

21. "LTVplus"
   Sourced from direct interview with Hawke Media Partner, LTVplus, 2021. For more information on LTVplus, see https:// www.ltvplus.com/.

22. "one of the fastest-growing marketing companies."
   Inc. 5000 2020. Inc.com. (2020). From https://www.inc.com/ inc5000/2020.

CHAPTER SEVEN

PRESS RELATIONS

When I was first starting Hawke Media, it was just me. I had a little bit of credibility because I had built and sold a few companies, but Hawke Media had no reputation whatsoever as a brand. Not surprisingly, one of my first clients was a friend. He started paying me to help with marketing, but a few months later, he said we needed to have a talk. I knew something was up.

He got straight to the point.

"Erik, I don't have a lot of money to pay you right now, but I love the progress we're making. I want you to do more. What else can we do?"

I had a decision to make. I could tell him that time is money and I needed to be paid for the time, or I could come up with another trade of value. And then the light bulb went off. He wasn't just a friend and an early client, he was a potential partner.

I knew the guy was a contributing writer for *Forbes*, so I said, "No problem. I understand money is tight. We'll find a way to partner on this and keep moving forward if you can feature my company in *Forbes*. Would that work?"

This was in 2013. *The Wolf of Wall Street,* featuring Leonardo Di Caprio, had just hit the box office. There was a ton of newfound excitement around *Forbes* as a publication, and a few weeks after our discussion, he published the article, "Why You Should Outsource your Marketing to Hawke Media."[23]

Immediately, from that moment on, Hawke had credibility. The article drove direct traffic from people googling *outsourced marketing, outsourced CMO*, and anyone looking at outsourcing parts of their business. To this day, we consistently get traffic from that article, published by a contributing writer in 2013. And it was all done through a quick relationship and positive press. You might think this brought us a ton of business right away, but that wasn't the case. The value was in the positive statements made by a trusted brand and etched into the mosaic of the internet forever.

THIS AIN'T YOUR MOM'S PR

PR is more about building trust than awareness. It's best used as a leverageable asset for other parts of your marketing strategy, not simply as a piece of news. Another Hawke Media partner, Richard Lorenzen, CEO of the New York PR firm, Fifth Avenue Brands, said it best. He told me:

> *"The true value of an effective PR campaign is the trust created when your brand is featured by a strong third-party news outlet. That trust pays dividends in perpetuity every time a prospect or an investor googles your company. Rather than just seeing ads and sales material, they now see an authoritative news outlet featuring your brand. What's more, these dividends compound significantly as you continue to leverage your brand's press recognition in all aspects of your branding and advertising, which increases your sales conversions and shortens the buying process."[24]*

Many established blue chip companies are still looking at PR through an antiquated lens. In the industrial age—the age of newspapers and magazines, radio and television—a big PR hit could be the reason your business succeeded. In the digital age, it doesn't work that way.

The internet and mobile phones have allowed information to flow effortlessly and instantly to people all over the world, which means there's a lot more of it. Videos, photos, articles, ads, press releases. There is so much stuff going into the world's content machine that a press hit doesn't get people's attention on a grand scale. One article is a blip on the radar in terms of awareness. People's attention is now distributed across more content. In fact, the signal-to-noise ratio is so low that a single piece of press gets lost in people's minds almost immediately. Since Hawke is a company that gets multiple quality press hits *per day*, I can tell you that the actual awareness element is negligible. But the ability to affect trust through PR is incredibly powerful. This is why we continue to spend on it.

WHEN PR WORKS, IT WORKS

You might remember when I spoke about launching my first e-commerce company in 2011, Swag of The Month, earlier in the book. When we were first starting out, we had no money. We couldn't spend on marketing, so I naturally started leaning toward the press.

I emailed the tip line at *TechCrunch*, and told them we raised some money. *TechCrunch* loved reporting early-stage raises at the time, and we knew that. They called me immediately, and an article about us was published that night.[25] Within hours, we got 600 people to subscribe to our new t-shirt subscription site: a single page that sent you off to PayPal to get a t-shirt every month. It was the first week of the business, and we were off to a good start.

Then I reached out to *Thrillist*. At the time, they were focused on being a men's publication. We sent them an email saying, "Guys hate shopping and we figured out a way to make it so guys don't have to shop anymore." They published a piece on us, too.[26] It said something along the lines of:

> *"There are a few better things in life than getting something in the mail, though one of them is definitely a hand job. For monthly packages that might just help get someone to touch yours, subscribe to Swag of The Month."*

That was published on November 14, 2011, and I thought it was hilarious. Then *Thrillist Los Angeles* picked it up, then London, then Boston, then their social media team picked it up, then *Maxim*, and then *The Wall Street Journal*.

It turned into a mini-phenomenon for us. We didn't know it at the time, but we had set up one of the first subscription e-commerce companies ever. Every men's publication was excited to talk about this new aspect of online shopping that was targeting men.

The main thing we realized from the experience is that you have to focus on what the journalist wants to deliver to their audience, not what you want to deliver. That is the best way to get press.

Make it easy on them. What headline and content do they want to write about? The cautionary tale here is everybody thinks they are interesting. We know you think your company is the greatest gift to the world, but why does the journalist's audience care and what is interesting about it? You'll notice that instead of a boring press release, or using a broad publication, we targeted *TechCrunch* and *Thrillist*, which were both highly relevant platforms. We knew their writers and audiences would be interested in what we were building, as opposed to trying to pitch *The Wall Street Journal* from the start.

To be fair, it is not a foolproof plan. And it's also a numbers game. You'll need to do a lot of outreach, but journalists are looking for good things to write about. That is their job. If you give them a relevant topic for their audience and a catchy headline, you've got a good chance that they will do it. Media companies are often cautious about being promotional, so you have to figure out how to avoid being salesy. For *TechCrunch*, we knew they wanted to write about fundraising, so the subject of the outreach email was, *"Swag of The Month raises $100,000 to stop guys from shopping."*

It caught their attention right away, and snowballed from there.

A good approach is to find top headlines on the target site and use a similar style. For *The Wall Street Journal*, it was *"An innovative business model on the Internet."* For *Elle*, it was *"How men are finding a new way to shop."* Helping your publication partners with the content is really important. After that, it's just a matter of reaching out and constantly hustling for it.

MAKE IT EASY FOR THEM

There are different ways for an article to get written and published. I have written an entire article draft, sent it to a journalist, and seen it published verbatim. Sometimes the journalist will edit it and add a couple of stats, essentially building from what I provide. In other cases, whatever is sent just gets them interested, and then they call me for a phone interview. Another popular option is an e-mail interview because nothing is taken out of context. The journalist will send me a list of questions and then create the article around my answers, using some of my responses as quotes, or they will just publish the entire written interview. Finally, some journalists will take it in their own direction and write their own article entirely.

What should you send to journalists? It depends. If you think you've got the article nailed for the publisher, write the article. But if you think they could do a better job, just write a paragraph and a headline to get their attention. If you write a whole article and they don't like it, you've lost them and wasted your own time. Whereas if you write a paragraph that's mildly interesting, they might give you a little bit of feedback. Quality and customization for the audience are critical.

RELATIONSHIPS MATTER, BUT CONTENT IS KING

With our PR, I am fortunate in that I'm seen as a thought leader. Publications will reach out to me asking for quotes and information. We do our own press releases to send out news about ourselves, and I'm also a contributing writer for a lot of publications.[27] I write for *Forbes, Entrepreneur, Fast Company, CSQ,* etc., so sometimes I am just writing articles because I am the journalist.

That said, I still have to run it by the editor, which is an important point to understand. I have columns with every major business publication and friends who hold high positions at those companies, but if the editor does not want to publish it, I'm out of luck.

Regardless of whom you know in the industry, if you don't have a compelling story, it won't get published. To land PR, you need good content, good salesmanship, and hustle. Your prior relationships can help, but there's no guarantee. This is why we caution against paying PR firms. Even if a PR firm has good relationships, it doesn't mean they'll be able to land press for you. You're paying a premium for their time, and they aren't going to hustle as hard as you. They also probably won't know how to angle the pitch as effectively, because it's not their business.

You would think the PR firm's personal relationships with media properties would counteract those downsides and that your article would still get published, but the relationship is not the critical element. That is not where the brunt of the work comes in. The brunt of work is in positioning the pitch and constantly coming up with new, interesting stories. That's the hard part. Doing this yourself, especially in the beginning, is a good idea. We often recommend keeping it in house and pulling in outside resources during big launches as necessary.

TACTICS FOR TOPICAL AUTHORITY AND SEO

For years, we've worked with Influence and Co. and Adogy. Influence and Co. helps us get columns with different publications like *Forbes* and *Entrepreneur*. Adogy, which is a company we still use, helps us link up with other contributors so we can write about things more indirectly. I write about the contributor's company and their clients, while they write about our company and our clients. We thereby create third-party validation, instead of Hawke writing about ourselves or our direct clients.

Adogy also considers SEO. We focus on content that performs well for our target search terms. When someone's searching for "*outsourced CMO*," the first thing that comes up is an article in *Forbes* about Hawke Media written by someone other than us. None of these strategies have anything to do with the audience of the article at the time of its release. It's about building long-term authority and trust by blanketing the internet with interesting, useful content over time.

WHERE IS THE TRAFFIC?

Clients often want to know how much traffic they can expect if they're mentioned in a big, mainstream publication. The answer is not much. At Hawke Media, we have built a massive PR machine. We get several PR hits per day. It could be a new award, an article that I wrote, an informative press release about our company's latest initiatives, news about our client's work, etc. Consider this: Even though we get several hits every single day—a lot of them in major publications—it drives almost zero traffic. Over time, we do see a small lift because people are finding those articles online through search. But the silver lining is this: The more articles there are to find, the more people eventually show up at your site. But that big bump from getting mentioned in *Inc.* or *Fast Company*? Those days wane quickly and are mostly over for Hawke Media.

CONTROLLING YOUR MESSAGE

In the digital age, PR is not a driver of awareness, despite my placing it within this section of the book. Yet, it is an invaluable asset and a way to control your message. We put it in the awareness section because of the common misconception.

By 2018, Hawke Media was growing significantly. We were a decent-sized business with over one-hundred employees and hundreds of clients. I was working on the sales side, and prospects would sometimes say things like: "Listen, we are deciding between you and this three-person agency run out of my nephew's garage. We're trying to figure out why you are better than them."

It was a big wake-up call for me. I'm thinking: "We've got one-hundred employees working on hundreds of contracts with top brands. How are we getting compared to your nephew and his two buddies in high school? What is going on here?"

Clearly the public didn't know we had scaled. I needed to control the dialogue more, so I called a friend who had a powerful position and said, "I want to be featured as one of the top five marketing consultancies in the country alongside the four other biggest players: Bain, McKinsey, BCG, and Accenture. Can we get that done?"

"I think you are nuts. Let me see what I can do."

This was one of those times I sent him the entire article, and he published it as a favor.[28] We shared it everywhere—to our email list, my social media accounts, our partners, and our clients—claiming that we were featured as one of the top five marketing consultancies in the country.

From a visibility standpoint, we were now in the top echelon of consultancies. And in response to clients considering small agencies over us, I started replying, "Are you serious? See this article."

It worked. We saw an immediate shift from those comparisons to concerns about our pricing and being too expensive to afford. Some potential customers were now priced out, but it put us into a higher market, which is where we wanted to be. Controlling our message helped us attract the right customers, which makes everything easier down the funnel.

HATERS GONNA HATE

All companies eventually get some haters—people who try to perpetuate a false narrative for whatever reason. You have to combat that. That's PR. It's part of doing business. Our PR partner you heard from previously, Richard Lorenzen, agrees:

> *"PR is just as much about controlling the spread of false, negative information as it is promoting the positive message of your products or services. The internet has opened the floodgates of slanderous information and fake reviews written about brands and public figures. Developing a documented strategy to control the narrative about your company is the PR team's most important function. Rather than just marketing, you are also playing the role of part-journalist, part-diplomat, and part-negotiator when communicating on your company's behalf with reporters and the public."[29]*

We heard some false narratives. For instance, that we hired all junior people and that our work was subpar. In response, we went full bore on reframing the narrative. We advocated that Hawke Media was the best place to work and has awesome employees. And we got third-party validation from our efforts by getting a bunch of awards after we showed how our training works, started highlighting our individual employees, and talked about their backgrounds and their wins. Rumors squashed.

To combat the rumor of subpar work, we did an initiative around case studies and getting awards for our clients. We got award after award after award, not for Hawke, but for our clients. This was a deliberate strategy to help us push the narrative in the right direction, highlighting all the amazing companies we support.

Guess who will now back us up when people try to say we don't do good work? That's right, our clients.

To me, guiding the narrative is part of the fun. It's also a good way to inform some of the things you should be doing at your company, because those negative narratives often come from a specific truth that then gets extrapolated or exaggerated. Fixing the problem, and then blowing it out with PR and showing you've fixed it, can be a powerful strategy. Then you can use that information as an asset. Talk about it in your advertisements, use it into your email marketing, in your content, and on your social media.

WHAT TO WRITE ABOUT

With PR, you ideally want to have a constant flow of interesting stuff to announce to the public, so you have to do newsworthy things. But don't think of it as news. Think of them as stories. If we weren't able to help our clients win awards, those would be real issues, and the haters would have been right. Thankfully, they were wrong. We just hadn't highlighted our wins enough. This gave us an obvious story arc to focus on.

PR is fluid. As you take the narrative in one direction, it opens up space for new narratives in new directions. For example, if we start talking too much about client success, people might lose sight of Hawke's *own* success, which could weaken our brand and put us back into the pot with all the other agencies. Then we would need to talk specifically about Hawke, our expansion, how we are different, our venture fund, and anything else that shines the spotlight on the company itself.

People have so much trouble figuring out what to write about. A good way to start is to ask: "What narratives do you want to either squash or highlight?" The answer to that question could just be your next press hit. One of Hawke's biggest clients was won by an opinionated, heartfelt article I wrote: "Get the Most Out of Your Marketing Agency in 5 Ways."[30]

I had gotten so sick of watching people waste my time, waste their time, and waste their money doing stupid things. They would hire me, but then they never did the proper things on their end to support our work and to actually get the most out of our services. I described how companies should work with an agency like ours if they wanted to succeed, stating plainly that it can't be adversarial. It must be a healthy, two-way relationship.

I published the piece in *Entrepreneur*, and then got a call from a guy named Michael Loeb. He told me he was looking for an agency to help with his businesses, and I was recommended by a friend. Then he was googling around and reading a great article about how to leverage an agency, and he realized it was written by me.

"So, Erik, it looks like we should work together," he said.

Michael Loeb is a multibillionaire, and he ended up being one of our biggest clients ever. It was a pleasure to work with him and it started with that initial piece of trust. He read my article and realized that it also aligned with his thesis and viewpoints. When you share your truths openly in print, and it aligns with someone else's values, you can immediately build some trust with your clients, even before the initial sales call.

THE PRESS SCHEDULE

At Hawke, we try to make a relevant PR announcement every week. It has to be impactful. It could be a big award, an initiative, an event, or a new partnership. This helps us reach new audiences, keeps us top-of-mind with our existing audience, and makes our customers feel more validated in working with us.

We typically do not announce when we're launching new lines of service because it's not a very interesting announcement. We do it individually with segments of our audience, but it's not a big, press-blitz approach...because who cares?

"Hey world, Hawke Media now does mass marketing."

Boring.

A partnership with the biggest SMS platform is interesting. A unique case study is interesting. An award is interesting.

KEEP THE MOMENTUM

People think of PR as outward facing, but PR has internal effects too. It helps your employees and partners stay excited about your business. When you are getting press hits, making announcements, building the brand, and controlling the dialogue, people inside the company feel it just as much as people on the outside.

Momentum is attractive. If you are constantly talking about new, exciting things at your company, people will want to be a part of it. They want to see momentum. They want to see progress. Everyone loves a good story.

KEY TAKEAWAYS

- Press can help with awareness, but it's not going to be the main driver.
- Press is not predictable in driving awareness, so it subsequently is not a reliable way to scale your business.
- Press is a good way to build trust and control the dialogue around your company.
- Press allows you to expound on your drive-by pitch with supporting material over time.
- Done properly, press provides third-party validation.
- Press is an asset, an ongoing drum roll that you probably want to continue banging on for the entirety of your business.
- It's important to strategize how you are going to use pieces of content being published by other parties. You should be leveraging third-party press in your advertising and within your own customer base as a nurturing mechanism.
- To figure out what to write about, ask yourself where you want the narrative of your company to go. What truths are not being highlighted enough? What misconceptions need to be debunked?

WANT TO LEARN MORE? Visit www.hawkemethod.com.

ENDNOTES

23. "published the article."
Pozin, I. (2014, April 23). *Leave it to the experts: Should you outsource your marketing?* Forbes. From https://www.forbes.com/sites/ilyapozin/2014/04/23/leave-it-to-the-experts-should-you-outsource-your-marketing/?sh=4222df242393.

24. "Fifth Avenue Brands."
Sourced from direct interview with Hawke Media Partner, Fifth Avenue Brands, 2021. For more information on Fifth Avenue Brands, see https://fifthavenuebrands.com/.

25. "article about us."
Constine, J. (2011, November 17). S*wag of the Month Raises $100k to Subscribe men to Indie Fashion.* TechCrunch. From https://techcrunch.com/2011/11/16/swag-of-the-month/.

26. "They published a piece."
Miller, J. (2011, November 14). *Because there's nothing better than a fresh shirt.* Thrillist. From https://www.thrillist.com/style/los-angeles/swag-of-the-month_online-shops_t-shirts.

27. "I'm also a contributing writer"
Visit https://www.erikhuberman.com/writing/ to view samples of Erik's writing.

28. "he published it."
Costarella, R. (2017, December 15). *Taking your marketing strategy to the next level might require a consultant.* Entrepreneur. From https://www.entrepreneur.com/article/293395.

29. "Richard Lorenzen."
Refer to source in note 24.

30. "Get the Most Out of Your Marketing Agency."
Huberman, E. (2016, February 18). *Get the most out of your marketing agency in 5 ways.* Entrepreneur. From https://www.entrepreneur.com/article/270446.

PART 2

—

Nurturing

CHAPTER EIGHT

NURTURING 101

Most people think of marketing chiefly as "getting the word out," aka advertising, which we're calling awareness in this book. But as you know by now, awareness is only one element—one leg of the tripod—and your marketing strategy won't stand on one leg. Marketing encompasses the entire lifecycle of a customer. What happens after someone sees the ad? What next?

In this section, we'll be talking about nurturing. Nurturing is what happens from the moment someone sees your ad to the moment they purchase your product/service—plus all the days, weeks, months, or years that follow—until they are no longer a customer.

The period between seeing an ad and making an initial purchase is called the purchase cycle or consideration period. If you nurture your prospects well, you can accelerate that period and entice them to buy sooner. Nurturing can also increase the rate of conversion. Your prospect may have seen the ad, but forgotten about it. Or, maybe they didn't forget, but there were other reasons why they weren't interested in buying yet and they needed more information. If you then nurture your customers after the initial purchase, they might buy from you again, which increases their lifetime value, or LTV. So even post purchase, you must continue to nurture your customers.

Advertising is competitive and costs have increased over the years. It's primarily based on a bidding system. The highest bidder wins the ad, so companies that generate the highest ROI from their ads can spend more and beat out the competition. And because there are a lot of companies doing this right, if your company is doing it wrong, you are going to lose. As advertising costs increase, your job is to increase lifetime value and conversion rate to counteract the cost and make your returns sustainable. That's where nurturing comes in.

AVERAGE PURCHASE CYCLES

This might be the most critical section in the book because it's the #1 mistake people make when analyzing their business. When you display an advertisement, most people who see it do not purchase your product on the spot. Observing hundreds of companies and products, we've seen that the average purchase cycle for a $50-order value in e-commerce is about three weeks. So it takes the average person three weeks to spend $50. For a $100 order, the average cycle is five weeks. For $200, it's an average of six weeks. It tapers off from there between two and three months for any type of large purchase or impulse buy.

If you're measuring the effectiveness of your advertising, and you're looking at your data on a week-by-week basis, you must account for the purchase cycle in your calculations. Clients will say to us: "We spent $10,000 today but we only made $3,000." Well, yes, but there's no need to panic. Because if you have a $50 retail value, you won't see the returns on that $10,000 for at least three weeks.

Learning this concept will stop you from cutting off your nose to spite your face. It also forces you to think about your nurturing strategy. If, on average, your customer is going to see an ad and then wait three weeks to make the purchase, what are you doing during those three weeks to ensure they actually buy? Can you push them to buy at a higher rate or accelerate their decision making process and get them to buy sooner? One important thing to remember:

"Time kills all deals."

Some very smart salespeople taught me that. Accelerating sales improves conversion rates. Make sure you are setting up your data analytics in accordance with your individual purchase cycle because I'm only giving you general numbers. Dig into the numbers for your own individual business and you'll learn, on average, how long it takes someone to buy your product from the first time they come to your website.

From there, set up your attribution and tracking methodology. Last step? Nurture the heck out of them.

FACEBOOK DATA MISCONCEPTIONS

We were working with a jewelry company and their average order value was $300. We were running Facebook ads for them and the business was doing well. But Facebook only reports data for a twenty-eight-day tracking period.[31] We wanted to implement another tracking system that would allow us to see beyond twenty-eight days, but they weren't interested. They only wanted to look at Facebook's reporting, because they were the behemoth in the industry.

The data didn't look good because we were spending $40,000 a month on advertising and Facebook was reporting an ROI of only $20,000 on those ads. And yet, the business was doing hundreds of thousands of dollars per month in revenue, showing a slightly positive trend over time.

I kept trying to coach the CEO: "Mike, we know you cannot see it in the existing data, but I promise you, with your price point, your purchase cycle is longer than twenty-eight days, so you won't see the full results from Facebook's twenty-eight-day tracking. We're still seeing healthy month-over-month revenue, and you aren't doing any other marketing whatsoever. Those purchases aren't coming out of thin air. This is working. We need more time and better tracking to see it in the data. Trust me on this."

When we tell clients we need three months to ramp up an advertising campaign to even start understanding trends and performance, it's not because we're slow or we can't put more people on it. It's because of the purchase cycle.

My business partner's favorite line is: "Nine women cannot have a baby in one month."

In other words, adding more people or more effort to a pregnancy doesn't speed it up. The same goes for marketing. You can do a few things to speed up your purchase cycle, but it generally takes time—sometimes months—if you have an expensive product. When someone goes through that cycle, we're still not done. That's just the cycle for one person. We need a bunch of people over a few months to go through this process so we can see the trend of dollars-in vs. dollars-out over time, with multiple cohorts. Only then can we begin to optimize which ads are driving purchases, so we can tighten our nurturing strategy, and increase ROI.

I'll reiterate: The two stats of your nurturing strategy that matter most are your conversion rate to initial purchase, and your LTV.

MAXIMIZING CONVERSION RATE

How do you increase the conversion rate from initial exposure to first purchase? There are lots of ways. During the consideration period, you should try to capture the prospect's email address. Then you can continue marketing to them through that channel.

But there is an art to this.

It's not: "Hey, I saw you clicked on one of our ads. Want to buy our product?"

That's the wrong approach, and you'll likely lose the prospect because that type of follow up is annoying. Instead, give them value propositions and address any common concerns so they better understand why they should purchase from you.

You can also retarget ads to increase your conversion-to-buy ratio. Have you ever gone to a webpage to consider buying something, decided not to purchase it, and then seen ads for it all over the place on other sites? That's retargeting.

When you visit a website, there's a good chance that site is using cookies. Cookies are tracking codes which allow the company to know you've visited their site. Now that company can use other tools like Facebook to show you more ads outside of their site's domain. The next time you open Facebook, you're confronted with an ad for the product you were just considering. This reminds the prospect to buy, but it can also create third-party validation, or at least the perception that the product is everywhere, making it feel more credible.

If you can collect the prospect's phone number, you can send text messages to help answer questions, or let them know about a special discount or sale.

Regardless of how you retarget, you should create engaging content for your audience that gives them a reason to look more deeply at your brand, ideally above and beyond a one-time-purchase decision.

MAXIMIZING LIFETIME VALUE (LTV)

As you know, the biggest driver of awareness is word-of-mouth, and the user's experience directly after their initial purchase will drive word-of-mouth more than anything else. When your customer experiences your product for the first time, they make a judgment call.

If you impress them, they'll want to share your product with their friends, so engaging with your customer post-purchase is critical.

In this scenario, you are nurturing your customer not only to affect their future purchase behavior, but to leverage them as a word-of-mouth foot soldier. As this marketing machine runs and more people enter your funnel, you can leverage various tools to continue nurturing your audience, including public content, email, SMS, social channels, events, and more.

Remember, time kills all deals. If you keep the audience engaged, you get more time with them. If you continue to nurture them, you can likely get a bigger share of their wallet over time, maximizing their LTV.

Our partner, LTVplus, specializes in scaling e-commerce businesses, so they know the ins and outs of nurturing customers. LTVplus co-founder and CEO, GQ Fu, said:

> *"We see an increase in conversion rates and customer retention when businesses adopt a proactive approach to customer service. By anticipating your customers' needs and reaching out to help them in advance, you create more pleasant experiences."*[31]

DON'T FORGET TO SEND FLOWERS

The Bouqs is an online flower company.[32] It's hard to get someone to buy flowers online. It's one of the most competitive markets because there are certain days when people are buying flowers, and all the players are vying for the same customers on those days. Mother's Day is the top sales day, Valentine's Day is the second highest. If you can't retain your customers and get lifetime value out of them, it becomes a very hard business because you're always fishing for new customers instead of pulling from your existing audience of nurtured prospects and customers.

So, The Bouqs had a great idea: set up a calendar system that would remind customers to buy flowers before specific holidays or birthdays. But they went a step further and included an option to run the whole process automatically. The system can select an appropriate bouquet, purchase it, and send it to the specified recipient on the specified day each year, without the customer lifting a finger.

Now, instead of one-off sales and frantic hunts for new customers throughout the year, The Bouqs was running an automated nurturing machine. They could take someone who bought flowers once on impulse and gently convert them into a repeat customer to increase purchase volume and LTV. And from the customer's point of view, it's a convenience. Convincing a customer to spend more than they would have spent originally is the holy grail of nurturing. If you master this, it means you can spend less on advertising and still get better results than your competitor.

You're squeezing more juice out of every orange, so to speak.

REMEMBER TO SHAVE MORE OFTEN

Dollar Shave Club entered the men's razor market as a nobody. They had zero market share and were up against blue-chip incumbents like Gillette, a company founded in 1901.[33] How were they supposed to compete against trusted brands that had been around for over a century?

Dollar Shave Club had an innovative business model. They touted the fact that you need to change your razor every week. Nobody had ever said that. People were not doing that. If you watch commercials prior to Dollar Shave Club coming to market, all the advertising for men's razors focused on quality. It was always about how the razor would last forever, or how it had eight blades, or a vibrating handle. No one was thinking about convenience.

When Dollar Shave Club sold for over a billion dollars, they accounted for 10% of the razor market.[34] Here's the funny thing about that stat: They didn't actually steal that much market share from the other companies. They created it. Instead of someone buying a razor every two months, they got their customers to buy every week. That's an 8x higher purchase frequency than their competitors' customers. So even if they only grabbed a few percent of the existing market, they were getting a much bigger share of those customers' wallets, and a much higher LTV.

Selling razors as a subscription service meant Dollar Shave Club could interact with customers on a regular basis, too. They could create content about how current razors are too expensive, and how guys should be replacing their dirty razors more often for a better shave. They ran an incredible ad on YouTube and did some effective television campaigns to build awareness, but the true success and longevity of Dollar Shave Club is in their nurturing machine.

IT'S IN THE AVERAGES, NOT THE ANOMALIES

People come to us all the time and say, "I need you to run my Facebook ads." After doing our research, we learn that the prospect has a terrible website, no email funnel, and no brand awareness or platform.

"You need to build a strong funnel before we start advertising."

"No, no, no. It's fine," they'll say. "We just want to drive people to the site right now, and we will see how they convert. We have an incredible product and need the revenue."

So, we run the ads, and of course, a month later, we get a call.

"We're not getting any sales. What is the problem?"

And begrudgingly we respond, "Most of the people who see your ad are likely watching it while they stand in line or go to the bathroom. They see the ad, click over to your unpolished website where you collect no information, and move on. And they never think about you or your product ever again."

You can't expect ads to magically drive sales. There are many other variables to consider before you can convert an ad impression into an actual purchase.

It's a highly competitive landscape, so there is always someone else doing all the right things. They're texting their prospects, emailing them, retargeting them. And you are not. You are spending the same amount of money and both competing for the same ad space. You're never going to see a return on that because the other competitor is doing all the right things, and you're both playing in the same sandbox.

Most marketing is logical. Look at yourself. Consumers see ads all day, every day. How often do you actually buy something from seeing a single ad for a product or brand you've never heard about? I'm talking about an impulse buy from an ad on Google or Facebook or Instagram. The chances are slim to none. It can happen, and it does. But when we're talking about a company managing its marketing, that individual anomaly is immaterial. Companies must build their strategy based on the global averages, and the averages say it will take weeks to sell your product.

Some founders think the way to launch their company is to start running ads. But if you haven't built a funnel, you'll spend that money and it won't drive profit.

There are usually two reactions from here. You either think your advertising channel is broken and won't work for you, or you think your product sucks and you fold the business altogether.

It's quite plausible that neither of those assumptions are true. It could just be that you didn't have the right follow-up method in place. Often, people prematurely shut down their businesses in these scenarios, or just don't profit from their advertising because they didn't set up the proper funnel.

PRO TIP: We often see this issue cropping up with the lean startup or Minimum Viable Product (MVP) methodology. Founders build a minimal product, but not a viable one. Nurturing is critical for viability because if you haven't created a funnel, measuring viability doesn't even happen. How will you know if a product is viable if you aren't doing anything to convert that prospect into a customer and drive lifetime value? Until you can accurately measure the returns from putting your product into the world and marketing it, you do not have a viable product. You have a minimal product, which will fail in most cases.

NURTURING BUILDS YOUR BASE

Acquiring customers is often the hardest task for a business and one of the biggest expenses, especially for early-stage and growth-stage businesses. If you want to make sure you are maximizing the returns on any awareness you are creating, nurturing is where you do that.

Through positive nurturing, you can actually sustain your business when awareness becomes too expensive or hard to scale. You can at least keep your existing base strong if your nurturing system is in place.

Nurturing is far less expensive than awareness. To build awareness, you have to keep spending. Most marketing expenses come in the form of advertising, endorsement deals, and sponsorships. Conversely, to maintain a good nurturing system, you simply have to build the system and then scale it incrementally over time. The cost of building out your CRM, your content calendar, and your email marketing funnel is the same now as it will be ten years from now—and the additional cost that comes with more customers is negligible. As an example, you should have an email marketing system in place to nurture your audience. To drive more customers into that system will cost far more than setting up and maintaining the system itself. To put it another way, as you scale your business, the cost of nurturing your audience gets lower, while its effectiveness gets higher. Setting up this infrastructure early, in an automated, evergreen way, will ensure the system scales.

NURTURING FROM DAY ONE

"We have a Minimum Viable Product so let's run ads and get some sales. We don't need to set up email marketing because we don't have any customers yet. And we don't need to start nurturing because we haven't started advertising yet."

If I'm your potential customer and you show me a Facebook ad, collect my email address, and then don't email me for two months, you've lost my attention. I don't even remember who you are anymore. My awareness is back to zero.

It is critical from the beginning, even for that first email subscriber, to have some automation set up. If you're just running ads and not nurturing, you're wasting your money. Your results mean nothing. There are very few cases where it makes sense to run ads without having automated nurturing set up. You should be testing how successful you're going to be, and to do that, you need all of the pieces of the machine working together.

Building awareness without having a nurturing system in place is like trying to catch a fastball without a mitt.

KEY TAKEAWAYS

- Nurturing is the marketing that happens after a prospect demonstrates awareness of your brand.
- The average purchase cycle for a $50-order value in e-commerce is about three weeks. For a $100 order, the average cycle is five weeks. For $200, it's an average of six weeks.
- Time kills all deals. Get to the sale as quickly as possible.
- Acquiring customers is often the hardest task for a business and one of the top expenses. Maximizing the return on every customer comes through nurturing.
- Through positive nurturing, you can sustain your business when awareness becomes too expensive or hard to scale.
- It is critical to nurture your prospects and customers from day one.

WANT TO LEARN MORE? Visit www.hawkemethod.com.

ENDNOTES

31. "LTVplus"

Sourced from direct interview with Hawke Media Partner, LTVplus, 2021. For more information on LTVplus, see https://www.ltvplus.com/.

32. "The Bouqs."

https://bouqs.com./

33. "company founded in 1901."

Lukas, P., & Overfelt, M. (2003, April 1). *Gillette in His Early Days.* CNNMoney. From https://money.cnn.com/magazines/fsb/fsb_archive/2003/04/01/341005/.

34. "Dollar Shave Club sold."

Wade, M. R. (2018, August 16). *Unilever buys Dollar Shave Club: A desperate or strategic deal?* IMD business school. From https://www.imd.org/research-knowledge/articles/unilever-buys-dollar-shave-club/.

CHAPTER NINE

CONVERTING CUSTOMERS

What can you do to increase the conversion rate from leads to purchases? In this chapter, we'll explore how to calculate your purchase cycle, how to stay in contact with prospects and customers, how to reinforce value propositions, and how to keep your brand top-of-mind.

Self-proclaimed marketers love to run Facebook ads and then take credit for the growth of a business. But they're not converting traffic, and they're not retaining that traffic. They're simply driving it in. Business owners often think there's a hole in the advertising strategy, when it's actually the conversion funnel.

I'm sure you've heard the expression, "You've got to spend money to make money." This is supposed to be the part where you make the money after spending it. But it only works if you do the conversion piece correctly.

Let's start with the purchase cycle, or consideration period. Remember, there's a period of time between seeing an ad and making the initial purchase. When you see a car ad, you don't rush to the dealership and buy the car in that instant. You take your time, research, visit a few dealerships, and then make a final decision. There are always exceptions. If you're Elon Musk and you see a commercial for a cool new car, maybe your assistant goes and buys it that day. But otherwise, you take your sweet time.

CALCULATING YOUR PURCHASE CYCLE

To calculate the purchase cycle for your company, you need to track two events:

1. The first time the customer engages with your brand through an ad or other awareness mechanism.
2. The first time the customer makes a purchase.

Over time, an average duration between the two events will emerge. This is your purchase cycle. Once you know the duration of the cycle, you can optimize that entire period for maximum conversion. You can do that using various tools like email marketing software, a high-converting website, and content marketing. One of Hawke Media's partners, Nitzan Schaer, is the CEO and cofounder of WEVO, a company that pinpoints why customers fail to engage. Schaer said:

> *"Seven-out-of-eight attempts to optimize conversion rates fail to have a meaningful impact. Companies should evaluate their websites with a customer-experience platform to optimize the digital experience and provide fast, accurate insights. This allows companies to pinpoint why more customers are not engaging, measure against industry benchmarks, and leverage actionable recommendations to drive more conversions during the purchase cycle."[35]*

VALUE PROPOSITIONS AS TALKING POINTS

Athletic Propulsion Labs makes awesome shoes. But they can't just tell their customers that. They need to demonstrate it. When a customer sees an ad for an Athletic Propulsion Labs sneaker, the company needs to continue nurturing the customer through the consideration period, which could take several weeks. To do this, they can focus on capturing email and then communicate value propositions using automated email marketing. For example, they can send an email about how their shoes were banned by the NBA because they make you jump so high. They can send another email a few days later highlighting various celebrities wearing their shoes, providing third-party validation and making the brand seem "cool."

When you apply this to your own business, think about what you can tell your customers to impress them, inform them, or persuade them to buy your product. Communicating in terms of value propositions doesn't feel salesy. It feels more like useful information.

CASTING YOUR NET

We've all seen banner websites. These are the sites with a section about the company, the product, the team, and a contact form. Unless you just want a website to make yourself feel good, what is the point of that? Everything should be intentional. Every piece of content on your site should guide your potential customer to a conversion. That doesn't mean you don't include the sections mentioned above. Some people will not buy without knowing more about you, or reading a FAQ. But you should be testing everything while picturing a funnel that covers all your bases. It becomes a net that guides customers down the funnel to the eventual sale.

The customer should always have an easy way to buy. Do you have a "Buy Now" button or a "Call Us" button? *You should.* It amazes me how many companies do not include these simple paths to a purchase. As your conversion data gets more refined, you can help your customer feel ready to make the purchase in more nuanced ways, through strategic communication. This takes trial and error. You'll eventually learn about your customer and understand the most common barriers to making the purchase. Then you can help alleviate those pressures.

Be careful, though. Too much information can actually be detrimental. You can give so much information that it becomes overwhelming and scares the prospect away. You need to give them exactly what they need to make an informed purchase decision and nothing more.

The moment someone signs up as part of your email list, they've told you they're interested in your product. They haven't purchased yet, but they're interested. Now you need to transform their interest into a decision to buy.

Different people are sold by different things. It is important to understand that you are going to require multiple value propositions. Some people will want to know more about the product and why it's great. Some people will want to see third-party validation. You need to offer all the value propositions that will handle the most common objections.

It could be quality. It could be trust. It could be the price point. Each email becomes a bite-sized piece of objection handling. One email covers third-party validation. Another email provides evidence around quality. As you understand your business better, and why people *didn't* buy, you can confront these concerns during the consideration period to continue optimizing your conversion rate.

DELETE YOUR FAQ

I remember we wrote a lengthy, informative FAQ for my t-shirt subscription company, Swag of the Month. We made sure customers could navigate directly from the FAQ page to the sales page so we could immediately capture those prospects as soon as they felt ready to buy. But when we looked at our data, we saw that a huge percentage of the people who went to our FAQ page never made a purchase. They would go to the FAQ page and then leave the site.

Even though, intuitively, you would think that an FAQ is always a good piece of content to guide customers down a sales funnel, that isn't necessarily the case. Apparently, the answers in our FAQ were not very good. We tried to tweak it, but it didn't help much. When we got rid of it completely, our conversion rates spiked. It was a strange realization, but for our business, people did not actually need an FAQ in order to buy. In fact, they were more likely to buy *without it*. Optimizing your funnel isn't always obvious. You have to look at your data closely and try different things.

THE BABY, THE BATH WATER, AND WINNING

Your prospect-to-purchase conversion rate sits within the second marketing principle of *The Hawke Method*, nurturing. This is a separate and distinct effort from driving awareness, which is the first principle.

Think of it as a unique part of your marketing strategy. We often see internal marketing teams blending the two, and then the company will throw the baby out with the bathwater, thinking their advertising isn't working when it's actually a poor conversion funnel, or vice versa.

Your consideration period and your conversion rate are the metrics you should be measuring to have full visibility into your funnel. If you optimize this well, your advertising dollars suddenly go much further. You can now spend less money on advertising and get a higher return. You'll be able to win, so to speak. If you don't do this well, your advertising might never work.

This chapter has highlighted the concept of the conversion funnel and how to optimize it for faster conversion and higher propensity to convert. But sight tight, in other sections, I'll talk in more detail about the specific *tools* for driving those conversion rates. There's one more element to optimize for the ideal nurturing strategy to be complete that we've only touched on. It's called lifetime value, or LTV.

KEY TAKEAWAYS

- Know your purchase cycle. The purchase cycle is the duration of time between the customer's first engagement with your brand, and the first time the customer makes a purchase.
- Use value propositions to entice customers to buy.
- The customer should always have an easy way to purchase.
- The more you optimize, the further your advertising dollars will go.

WANT TO LEARN MORE? Visit www.hawkemethod.com.

ENDNOTES

35. "WEVO."
Sourced from direct interview with Hawke Media Partner, WEVO, 2021. For more information on WEVO, see https://www.wevoconversion.com/.

CHAPTER TEN

INCREASING LIFETIME VALUE

The Bouquet Bar was a flower company with a unique product offering. They sold a giant orange gift box with a bouquet of flowers and assorted candies. It might sound status quo, but this thing was massive, and beautifully presented—the type of gift that would definitely impress. I even bought one for my wife and she loved it!

The Bouquet Bar was featured on the popular television show *Shark Tank*, so naturally they were receiving a bunch of awareness.[36] They also had multiple press hits driving traffic to their site. And people were buying.

They hired us to scale the business, but we immediately noticed a problem. It would be difficult to drive repeat purchases. Once you give this gift to someone, you can't really give it to them again next year or even for a different occasion because it's very novel and specific. It would feel like getting the same gift twice. And to buy the gift more than once for different people would be rare too: it was a high-priced product relative to other competing products in the market. People usually spend that kind of money on their closest relationships, or for a significant life event. In other words, it was kind of a gimmick, and from a business perspective there wasn't much longevity in it.

The other issue was word-of-mouth. Think of it from my perspective. I bought it for my wife, but I wouldn't tell my friend to buy it for *his* wife, because our wives talk. I can hear my wife now:

"Erik, what were you thinking? You guys got us the same gift? Seriously? How original."

She'd have a point. The novelty of the gift actually ended up being the problem. And the overarching problem was that it reduced the lifetime value of every customer to a single purchase. They were running a one-hit wonder business.

Sadly, Bouquet Bar didn't last. They eventually had to shut down because they didn't build their business in a sustainable way that would increase LTV.

TRUE ROI

If you talk to a finance person or anyone who may want to buy your company, they'll want to know your True ROI (tROI). This is your return on investment for the marketing dollars you spend. To calculate your tROI, you divide your customer's average LTV by your average cost to acquire that customer (CAC).

$$tROI = LTV / CAC$$

If your tROI is higher than one, you can generate a profitable ROI on your marketing spend. This is truly how to scale a company.

IS MY TROI GOOD ENOUGH?

Typically, you should aim for a tROI of 4x or higher. In other words, you should eventually make at least $4 for every $1 spent on marketing. Keep in mind, these are ballpark figures assuming a healthy gross margin of 50% or higher.

In private equity, a tROI of 6x or higher is considered favorable. Obviously, the bigger the better. If your tROI is really big—like 20 or 30x—it usually just means you're not taking enough risk on marketing. You should be spending more and scaling faster. You don't need to make that much of a return.

TRICKY COHORT ROI MATH

Different marketing campaigns create cohorts with unique behaviors, which means they need their own unique analysis and tROI calculation. For example, let's say you are advertising on both Television and Facebook. Your CAC on Television ads is $30 and your CAC on Facebook is $60 dollars. Does this mean Television is the better option? Not necessarily.

Imagine this breakdown: The TV ads are driving one-time customers who have an LTV of $150. The $150 is captured in the first month. On Facebook, ads are driving more loyal customers. Their LTV as a group is $300, but captured over a year.

A junior marketer might say, "The CAC is higher on Facebook. Cut it off."

An intelligent marketer would say, "Look at the cohort analysis. Over time, we're getting better returns on our Facebook campaigns than we are on TV. We should double down on Facebook, even though the initial cost is higher."

WHY ROAS IS BS

A popular metric we hear all the time in advertising is ROAS (pronounced "roh-ahz"), or Return on Ad Spend. In a vacuum, this is a ridiculous metric. Many companies look at this number on a weekly basis without taking into account their customer's purchase cycle or LTV. They completely cut off their marketing because they think it's not working, but they're only looking at Return on Ad Spend, which doesn't paint the whole picture. The ad, as we know, is only the first leg of the journey. ROAS means nothing if you aren't looking at it in context with your customer's consideration period and LTV.

Let's use Dollar Shave Club as an example again. Let's say their average customer spends $5 a month. To acquire a customer, it costs them $15. That looks really bad in terms of ROAS in the first month. They spent $15 and only made $5. Should Dollar Shave Club shut down? Are they screwed? Of course not.

Remember, Dollar Shave Club is a subscription service, so customers are expected to continue paying each month. If the average monthly spend is $5, we need to know how long that customer continues to pay. Is it three months, six months, a year? Let's say the average customer spends $5 per month and the bulk of customers continue to pay for twelve months. Now we know our customer's lifetime value is actually $5 for twelve months, or $60. Not $5.

So even if Dollar Shave Club spends $15 on each customer they acquire, they make $60. They just don't make it right away. It takes a year. This is okay. Now the only issue is having enough working capital to make it through the year. If they won't see the full $60 for twelve months, they just need enough cash to operate the business as more money rolls in. If this becomes an issue, they can consider raising capital to give them a buffer, or even increase ad spend to accelerate growth. This is exactly what Dollar Shave Club did, and it's one of the reasons they grew so quickly and captured a significant market share before the incumbents could copy them.

DETERMINING LTV

There are different theories about how to calculate the most accurate Lifetime Value. Our method at Hawke Media is focused on finding a number that is both representative of your customers' buying behaviors and useful for your business. We do this by looking at cohorts. A cohort is a group of people who purchased your product. You can group people in different ways, but one of the most common approaches is to use various time periods. For example, you could create a cohort of all the customers who made their first purchase yesterday. Once you've defined a cohort, you can track their behavior as a group over time.

These groupings are helpful because the data can get muddled if you lump everyone together. For instance, if you take the LTV of a customer who made their first purchase for $5 yesterday, and you average it with another customer who has made multiple purchases totaling $100 over several years, are you really getting an accurate LTV figure by averaging the two together? Probably not. It's quite likely that the new customer will buy again, which would lift the average LTV. And the veteran customer still might spend again too, even though it has been 5 years. How do we reconcile these time-dependent variables to find an appropriate and representative LTV?

First, let me tell you what not to do: use a very long period to calculate your LTV. If you tried to calculate LTV over a five-year period, you would need at least five years of business to get your stat in the first place! You may also start to see extreme outliers that cause over-reporting issues. And finally, do you really need to forecast five years into the future to run your business well? No.

I advise early-stage companies and SMBs to track their LTV assuming a one-year total lifetime. This makes sense because purchases made five years into the future won't help me grow my business today. And I probably haven't even been up and running for five years if I'm a startup. Realistically, I only need to know what I'm earning over the next twelve months so I can forecast my runway.

When you're small, your entire life as a company should be viewed in chunks of one year. This is a healthy average age for most startups to die. If you map your customer's total lifetime to your worst-case, death scenario, your LTV will be conservative, which I think is smart. As you grow, you can analyze bigger cohorts over longer periods to get more refined data.

LTV can change significantly when viewed over longer periods, but you have to think about making the stat relevant to your business now. Imagine a car company. If I am a brand new car company, even if I expect to sell the same customer a new car every ten years, that second car purchase in my tenth year doesn't help me now. I only need to worry about the first purchase to forecast my first several years in business.

Ferrari says they market to five-year-old children to sell them at thirty-five. It's hard to measure that, but that's okay because for bigger brands. It's not always about direct data. Sometimes these periods are longer than you can actually measure in tangible datasets and you have to be a little more broad-scoped or make a few assumptions. Mid-to-late-stage companies often use a lifetime of three years to determine LTV.

It is important to look at multiple cohorts, some that are further back in time and some that are more recent, so your cohort data doesn't get stale. Your company may have improved over time, so newer cohorts could be performing better and have a higher LTV than older cohorts or vice versa. Multiple cohort analysis is a great way to track positive and negative trends in your marketing strategy over time.

OPTIMIZING LTV

It might blow you away...but the #1 strategy for optimizing your LTV is to have an awesome product or service. It is remarkable how many companies blame their marketing efforts or something else for people not buying their product, when in reality they just have a bad product and nobody cares about it.

A good marketer can get a consumer to buy something once. But when the consumer buys and it's awful, they'll never buy from that company again. And that customer definitely won't be recommending it to anyone else. If you want to drive word-of-mouth and LTV, you must first have a great product or service.

Assuming you have a great product, you also need to stay in touch. I've seen so many companies that acquire customers and do nothing after that, assuming the customers will just come back when they're ready to purchase again. That is not how people behave. In some ways, people are very simple. If you remind them how much they like your product at the right time, they are going to buy more of it more often.

By analyzing purchase patterns, you can create targeted, automated email outreach and soft-selling opportunities. If a customer bought a shirt, maybe you should send them an email about the pair of pants that match it or a nice pair of shoes. If they haven't been back to your website in three months, they probably forgot about you.

Tell them you miss them! There are automated solutions to make sure you are staying engaged with your customers. This is also where content can become valuable. If you can keep people engaged with your brand above and beyond a purchase decision, they're going to remember that they like your brand the next time they want to buy. Realistically, I'll likely ignore an invasive ad about your sunglasses if it diverts my attention from what I was doing. But if I'm already on your site because I'm engaging in your fun content, and then I see a post about the sunglasses, I might be more likely to purchase. It's an entirely different experience.

LTV is also optimized by building the community around your brand. I was recently watching a MotoGP motorcycle race. During the race, one of the racers crashed and broke his arm. Six days later, he tried to race again with metal plates and screws in his arm. He was wearing a Red Bull helmet. That hit home as to why Red Bull is such a marketing powerhouse. People live by the brand. The Red Bull brand is so deeply entrenched with their customers and audience. This is not just about conversion; it's about keeping your community involved and engaged.

Nike is another great example of this. I doubt there's an NBA fan who hasn't bought a pair of Nike shoes. Every time Nike does another shoe deal with a franchise NBA player, their existing customers think: "Those are cool. Maybe I'll buy those!"

It's another touchpoint. That community has been trained to buy Nike shoes through consistent releases with franchise players over time. And when it's a franchise player you like, the urge is even stronger. These marketing campaigns are not just created with the mindset of selling a single product. They're created around the concept of nurturing the customer base to increase lifetime value.

To summarize, your LTV-to-CAC ratio is the most important metric to inform your marketing. We typically look at a one-to-three year timespan. If you can consistently and predictably drive your CAC down and your LTV up, your business will flourish. In a situation where advertising costs are increasing, you'll still be able to compete. And if you become so efficient that you can increase your spend, you'll outbid your competitors and skyrocket. A 4:1 ratio is sustainable. Anything over a 6:1 ratio is impressive.

KEY TAKEAWAYS

- *True ROI* is your actual return on investment for the marketing dollars you spend.
- *ROAS* stands for Return on Ad Spend. This stat isn't always useful because most companies don't consider their purchase cycle.
- Typically, you should aim for a tROI of 4x or higher. (You should eventually make at least $4 for every $1 spent on marketing.)
- Cohort Analysis can show us the Lifetime Value of a particular set of users over time.
- I advise early-stage companies and SMBs to track their LTV assuming a one-year total lifetime.
- You can optimize your LTV by displaying targeted upsells, building a community, and establishing trust.

WANT TO LEARN MORE? Visit www.hawkemethod.com.

ENDNOTES

36. "television show Shark Tank."
Fuchs, K. (Director). (2018) Season 9, Episode 19. Burnett, M. (Producer), *Shark Tank.* Los Angeles: Sony Pictures Studios.

CHAPTER ELEVEN

TOOLS & TACTICS

Here's where we take the time to get out of the abstract and into direct application. Knowing what mediums to best reach and nurture your customers is crucial to executing on your marketing strategy.

EMAIL MARKETING

When I talk about email marketing as a tool for nurturing, I'm talking about the email list you curated through your *own* leads and customers. I'm not talking about buying lists.

In 2010, I heard industry chatter that millennials don't use email, and that email as a technology is dead. Then in 2020, I heard the same thing about Gen Z. I'm a millennial, and I use email every day. The stats on Gen Z are going up now as well. After being in the industry for over a decade, I realized that children and high school kids rarely use email. They use other platforms, and those platforms fall in and out of favor every five-to-ten years. Some colleges actually don't require email, but most college students use it. And once you're in the working world, everybody uses email.

Our statistics at Hawke Media back this up. Email marketing hasn't gotten better, but it hasn't gotten worse either. The average open rate is still 15% and the average clickthrough rate is still 3% across the board.

Email marketing drives about 25% of revenue over time for all e-commerce, a multitrillion-dollar industry, where most businesses need to have some presence.[37] In fact, email marketing experienced a resurgence in 2020. Omnisend, an e-commerce marketing platform, found that conversion rates skyrocketed throughout 2020 compared to the year prior.[38] Promotional email campaigns netted a 111% year-over-year improvement. And just by incorporating a good, email-welcome series, conversion rates can improve by 50% to 300%. There's even an opportunity to boost sales through order and shipping confirmations. The conversion rate for these transactional messages jumped 346% from 2019 to 2020.[39]

If you're wondering whether you should be doing email marketing or not, the answer is almost always *"yes"* because the cost is very low. The cost scales with growth, but it's a negligible amount of money compared to the revenue you can drive from it.

CAPTURING EMAILS

Email works perfectly for nurturing your customer during the purchase cycle. We sometimes get pushback from clients who don't want an email-collection box to pop up on their site. They think it's annoying, and they use anecdotal evidence of people not liking it. But there are simple stats to judge whether or not you should have an email collection pop-up.

It would be apparent in your bounce rate. A bounce rate shows when people come to your site, get annoyed, and leave immediately. If you add an email collection pop-up to your site and your bounce rate goes through the roof, there is something wrong. In general, people are more willing to provide their email these days because they know they can unsubscribe whenever they want. You can probably convince 10% or more of your traffic to give you their email using a pop-up or collection form, which means you can now nurture those website visitors and guide them through the purchase cycle.

THE WELCOME SERIES

The first email marketing content we create with clients is called a welcome series. When someone gives you their email address, you should send them a welcome email. Try to create some value in it. Give them another reason to buy. Many companies offer a special discount on the first purchase when the consumer subscribes to their email list. There are other ways to do it, but the main goal is to provide a bit of value and an incentive to buy right away. The welcome email ranked as the highest converting automation email of 2020 at 51.9%.[40]

After the welcome email, you should set up an automated series of additional emails that are sent during your purchase cycle. The sequence can actually decelerate a little bit to avoid annoying the customer. Let's say your purchase cycle is three weeks. You may want to send the welcome email right away, then another after two more days, then another after four more days, then another after five more days, and then another after nine more days.

The idea is to stay in touch throughout the purchase period, keeping the frequency low, but giving them various reasons to buy. Each email should focus on a new value proposition. One email could be a statement of quality. Another could be highlighting your best selling items. The next could link to some positive press about you. People buy things for different reasons. After collecting enough data, you'll be able to see which emails lead to the most sales and put those first in the sequence. You can also keep tweaking the language in those emails to optimize conversions even further.

THE ABANDONED CART

The customer was about to make a purchase. They're on the checkout page, and they leave the site with something still in their cart. If the customer is on the checkout page, that indicates a high level of intent to purchase. Follow up with them right away.

It can be as simple as an email that says, *"Hey, you left stuff in your cart. Don't forget to check out! If you have any questions, reply back and we'll help you out."*

You can offer a discount in your follow-up email if you want, but be careful. Discounting too heavily or too frequently can devalue your product and train your customer to wait for discounts before buying. This message works. It's called "The Abandoned Cart" Email.

In data gathered by Hawke Media, Cart abandonment emails generated a 33.9% conversion rate in 2020. Among all other automated email types, the abandoned cart variety picked up the most steam as the year wore on. Its conversion rate catapulted twenty-one percentage points.

THE WINBACK

If someone hasn't visited your site, opened one of your emails, or made a purchase in a while, send them a winback email. This is an attempt to 'win back' their business. Called the "Lapsed purchaser" email, they are worth considering. In 2020, 21.27% of these emails resulted in a purchase.

This can be a super simple message, *"We miss you. Come back."*

You can also offer some kind of special perk or discount within this email as well. This note should be scheduled around the end of your average repurchase rate. For example, you can set up your email marketing software to send a winback message automatically to any disengaged customer who hasn't made a purchase in about five weeks, assuming that's approximately your average repurchase rate.

SEGMENTATION VERSUS EMAIL BLASTS

Don't blast your entire email list all the time. It's a bad strategy. If I buy something today and you send me a massive discount coupon tomorrow, I'm going to be irritated. Instead, segment and automate everything based on people's purchase decisions and behavior. If someone bought something within the past week, do not send them a discount. Everything should be automated because then over time, as you build your email list, it doesn't become a hamster wheel. Big announcements, roll up digests, and time-related events can be done through large email blasts. Those types of emails can be sent every so often. But most of your email should be automated based on people's behavior. Utilizing automated emails, such as a welcome series, abandoned cart message or a "happy birthday" wish, for example, is a wise choice. In 2020, they accounted for 1.8% of email sends but drove 29% of all email marketing sales.[41]

You want to create as much conditional one-on-one communication as possible. The more personalized you can get, the more efficacy you'll see out of your marketing. If you feel relevant, communicative, and personal when talking to the customer through email, there will be a higher propensity to act. Automating this means you must be highly strategic. You can test your automations and make iterative improvements. Over time, you can build out different funnels based on people's behavior. It starts with communication that reaches large segments, and then you can gradually get more and more narrow.

For example, you can create a specific email sequence for your top 10% of purchasers. You can send them specific deals or specific content that makes them more engaged. You can start to segment to different buckets based on lifetime value, the last time they purchased, how long they've been in the funnel, etc. With this iterative, data-driven approach, your email marketing becomes more powerful as you grow your business.

PRO TIP: This pro tip is courtesy of one of Hawke Media Partners, Klaviyo, a company that offers fantastic tools for email automation, and it plugs right into most e-commerce platforms. Their Head of Product Marketing, Jake Cohen, has prudent advice on owning your audience.

"People use lots of channels to connect online. They use social channels like Facebook, Instagram, and TikTok, and they use owned channels like email and text messaging.

Owned channels differ from social or paid channels because you have a direct relationship with your audience. You own the relationship. On the other networks, the platform owns the relationship. They decide which brands consumers get to communicate and connect with.

Creating a business is hard enough, and being subject to changing rules from third-party platforms makes it harder to succeed. When businesses can't reach their followers because the distribution of content is restricted, it's harder to succeed. When ad rates unpredictably go up, or display algorithms change, it's harder to succeed. The best way to build a lasting business is to own relationships with your audience. And the best way to do that is to connect with your audience on owned channels, like email and text messaging." [42]

EASE OF USE OVER ROBUST FEATURE SETS

When choosing an email marketing software, you should factor in your specific needs for your current growth stage. Is it easy to use?

We often see startups integrating robust, enterprise-level systems, but they can't leverage them properly because they don't have a development team. Some of the enterprise-level systems require a full marketing and development team to integrate and maintain properly. Even if you're making $10,000 a month, you probably can't afford to hire a full team to support the software. Focus on usable software for your stage of growth, and level up to enterprise systems later.

SMS MARKETING

SMS is 10x more effective than email marketing. And I'm not just saying that. There are statistics to back it up. Remember, email marketing has an average open rate of 15% and an average clickthrough rate of 3%. For SMS, the average open rate is 98%. This sounds awesome, but it's not surprising. When you get a text message, you open it to see who it's from. The more important stat is the clickthrough rate, which is a whopping 30% on SMS. Comparing email to SMS, the clickthrough rate jumps from 3% to 30%—a tenfold increase.[43]

It's a little harder to convince someone to give you their phone number vs. their email address, but it's not even close to 10x harder, so SMS can certainly be a powerful addition to your marketing strategy toolkit. The most valuable use case for SMS, in my opinion, is proactive customer service.

Let's say you're a boutique shoe company and someone leaves a pair of shoes in their cart. Shoes fall into the fashion category, and fashion is a tricky business online because the customer can't wear the item before buying it. If I'm considering buying shoes from your company and I don't know how they're going to fit, I'm not going to read your size chart, measure my foot, and read your FAQ. I don't care enough about your shoe brand to do all that. I'll leave your website and go buy some Nike shoes on Amazon.

Now is your opportunity to step in and close the sale. Through SMS, you can reach out to the customer as soon as they abandon their cart with an automated message. Put yourself into the mindset of the customer now. Imagine getting this text message as soon as you leave the website:

"Hey, Erik! We see you're interested in our new sneakers that debuted at Fashion Week in New York City. Did you have any questions about the shoe before you buy a pair?"

This is a feel-good message. It's not annoying. It's helpful. It also casually includes some credibility and gently suggests that the customer should make the purchase. You'll need a customer-service team standing by, but now the customer can respond and you can drive home the sale with a one-on-one conversation.

"Thanks. I like the look of your shoes, but I wasn't sure if I would be a size 10 or size 11."

"No problem. We run a tad small, so I would suggest sizing up to an 11. Also, we have free returns, so if it's the wrong size, you can always return it within thirty days as long as it's still in the box and hasn't been damaged or worn. Should I go ahead and place your order?"

Notice the subtle, proactive objection-handling? This is an easy sell to close. It's proactive customer service and it engages your customer in a way that feels good. Oisin O'Conner, Co-Founder and CEO of Recharge, a text-based customer experience tool says:

> *"Transactional SMS enables merchants to communicate with customers via text and let them know when their order is shipping and gives them the option to swap products, skip a shipment, or increase their order right from their phone. With RechargeSMS we are seeing an upward trajectory of LTV and AOV when these methods are used."*[44]

This works especially well with younger generations, who are getting accustomed to this type of interaction. With SMS, you can typically text "STOP" to stop receiving texts, and people are getting used to that, so they're becoming more comfortable providing their phone numbers. This is one of the fastest growing and most powerful marketing channels we've seen.

Our favorite tool for SMS marketing is Postscript. Full disclosure: We directly invested in the company. Their revenue jumped 6x in less than a year after we invested, and it has become one of the top partners to Shopify. We're very happy with Postscript as a partner. It has become one of our top services at Hawke Media because it's such an easy strategy to increase conversion and sales.

When I asked President and Co-Founder of Postscript, Alex Beller, about the benefits of SMS marketing, he said:

> *"Our blended ROI from 2020 for our customer was 32x. SMS is the next big thing for commerce, especially given the continued importance of owned marketing and the crowdedness of other channels like email. With SMS, brands have a unique, once-a-decade opportunity to connect with customers in a new way."* [45]

PRO TIP: People text their friends and their family. Now, brands have an opportunity to join that communication channel. You can't be spammy. But if you send text messages that feel authentic and personal, your customer will feel a more personal connection with your brand. It's a fragile but highly effective way to nurture your customers and build a relationship.

CONVERSATIONAL MARKETING

Customers no longer expect one-off messages in their inbox about a new promotion or product. They crave connection. With most consumers now shopping online, they're missing the experience of getting to engage with a store associate, sharing their pain points and having someone share personalized recommendations.

For brands struggling to build these deep, customer relationships, a company called Octane AI says there is a solution: conversational commerce.

The goal of conversational commerce is to bridge the gap between brand and consumer, helping them build strong connections by engaging with customers quickly, in a personalized way.

Put yourself in the customer's shoes for a minute. When you're shopping online with your favorite brands, how important is it for you to have a direct line to be able to connect with stores to ask questions, receive personalized content and recommendations, ask for shipping updates, and discover great products? Having a quick way to connect is critical for maximizing the customer experience.

One of the best platforms to connect with customers is Facebook Messenger. Why? Not only are customers able to respond and have back-and-forth conversations with brands, but compared to all the messaging platforms available, Facebook Messenger ranks as one of the most popular platforms. Basically, Facebook Messenger is your first-class ticket to disproportionately high open rates, clickthrough rates, and conversions.

Ben Parr, President and Co-Founder of Octane AI, says:

"Conversational Commerce offers a better way to shop online. With AI technology, brands can build a relationship where the right products and information can be

shown at the right times. The results are undeniable. At Octane AI, we've seen brands successfully drive 80-95% open rates, 43% average clickthrough rates, and a 7-20% increase in revenue using our Facebook Messenger campaigns and flows."[46]

With a bit of personalization and direct communication with customers, your brand can see results like this too.

Building automated flows and campaigns on Facebook Messenger can help you accomplish several things with minimal effort on your team's end:

- Respond to common customer questions and inquiries in real-time with an automated chatbot.
- Follow up with customers after they abandon their search or their carts to remind them about products they were interested in.
- Use automation to ask customers questions about their challenges and pain points to automatically offer them a solution.
- Send customers order confirmations and shipping updates so they can easily track their orders.
- Use Sponsored Messaging to send conversational ads that feel more personalized and engaging than the standard Facebook ad.

Remember, customers are looking to connect and engage with brands in a personalized way. Using the channels they interact with most and sending them content they're interested in is the first step to building a loyal customer base that continues to grow.

CHATBOT MARKETING

Another effective strategy for proactive customer service is through chatbots. In many cases, people just want to talk to someone really quick. The one-on-one interaction is super helpful. With chatbots, you can automate it over time as you collect the standard questions people ask. Octane AI is the tool we use for this, but remember to do your own research and use the tool that fits best with your unique business.

CONTENT MARKETING

There's a multibillion-dollar company that sells a relatively unhealthy drink to its customers without spending a dime on advertising. You've heard me mention them before: The company is called Red Bull. I've alluded to them several times in this book because they're on the cutting edge of content marketing strategy. Instead of advertising, they create tons and tons of content.

When I'm watching race car videos, dirt biking videos, and snowboarding videos, Red Bull is everywhere. Now the craving starts. It's as if they inject demand into their existing audience through life experiences. They become a part of their customers' daily lives. This is more subtle than an ad, and seeing Red Bull doubling down on it would suggest it's also far more effective. In a time of health-consciousness, Red Bull is still skyrocketing without running ads, and their media company is actually turning a profit. Instead of spending money on advertising, Red Bull can nurture their audience through relevant content and make money in the process.

At Hawke Media, we focus on providing accessibility to great marketing for everyone. Our content is targeted to the people who need our services, which are generally business owners and entrepreneurs. As your digital-content footprint grows, it develops into thought leadership. We cover various relevant topics for segments of our audience, like startups, venture capitalists, etc.

For your business, you should be bucketing your audience into relevant topical areas and then creating content for those audiences. Don't get too far away from your core business. For example, we don't create content about tax liability at Hawke Media because it's outside our area of expertise and it therefore wouldn't be targeting our core audience.

Let's take the example of swimwear. If you sell swimwear, you need to create content to complement the product. What is the aspiration behind the product and what else surrounds that aspiration? If I'm buying a swimsuit, what else might I be interested in? You could talk about the best beaches in the world, travel tips, fitness, nutrition. All of those topics relate back to the product in a fun and useful way. Whether this content is being consumed by a lead who hasn't converted yet, or an existing customer, you're keeping them engaged without hard-selling them. The relationship is no longer merely transactional, it is now relational.

Content marketing can propel your word-of-mouth strategy too. As you would expect, people like sharing content much more than ads or discounts. Going back to the running shoe company example, you could publish an article about the top ten running trails around the country. I'm more likely to share that article with my running buddies than a coupon code. Now my friends are reading the article while also being subtly introduced to your brand and products. This introduces people to your company without being spammy or salesy because you're actually providing value beyond the product. You are giving them something instead of simply taking their money.

Content marketing also gives you an opportunity to highlight your company's personality. If you do this well, it makes people feel more aligned with you. Tell people who you are and what you stand for. Patagonia is a good example. They consistently publish content around the things you can do to help the environment, and they take action. They've bought millions of acres in South America and turned it into protected land. People buy from Patagonia not just because they need a jacket or a suitcase, but because they love what the brand represents. In this way, content marketing can become a differentiator.

Why should you buy from one company over another? Patagonia gives its customers a clear reason, without shouting it. It's a subtle whisper that keeps reminding you.

When it comes to differentiation and the strategy behind your content marketing, you can be deliberate in your approach based on the competitive landscape. 5-Hour Energy is an interesting example that relates back to Red Bull. Red Bull has a stronghold on the adventurous, adrenaline-driven audience. It would be hard for 5-Hour Energy to compete from that angle. Do you see 5-Hour Energy logos on any race cars? No. And that's deliberate. That's Red Bull's territory and they know it. Other energy drinks have tried to compete with some success, but Red Bull is still the juggernaut.

5-Hour Energy took a completely different approach. Their marketing focuses on the 2:00 p.m. slump at work. Their audience is the tired business person trying to power through another day at the office. Remember their commercials of people passing out on the job? 5-Hour Energy went after the business professional, which was presumably a deliberate marketing choice. You can choose where you want to take your content marketing and how you want to build authority to stake your claim, find your place in the market, and get your piece of the pie.

LOYALTY PROGRAMS

People love games. Most games use levels to keep the player engaged, and compulsion loops to bring the player back. These are called game mechanics, but they work in any industry. Using gaming principles in other industries is known as gamification, and you've likely experienced it in the business world in the form of loyalty programs.

I often use DoorDash instead of Postmates simply because I accrued some bonus coupons toward my next purchase. Then they got me hooked on the free delivery subscription, so now I always choose them. They won my loyalty through a simple gaming tactic. American Express is another good example. Their point system is so powerful and has benefited me in so many ways that I always edge toward paying with my Amex. All of the frequent flyer programs are also loyalty programs using the concept of gamification to win business and drive loyalty.

Every loyalty program is unique. Hawke Media Partner, Smile.io is an expert in rewards programs. They say:

> *"When the objective of loyalty is to bring the customer back to your store, determining the exact percentage back is not a one-size-fits-all situation. Businesses with high purchase frequency can be successful with a 1-2% back structure, but most businesses will land in the 3-10% range. To find an appropriate range, consider your average order value, purchase frequency, and margins. If it takes too long to accumulate points, your program won't drive repeat purchases. A good rule of thumb is to offer your customers enough points to redeem them for a reward after their second or third purchase."* [47]

A company called Westside Wholesale was a Home Depot competitor that didn't have any brick-and-mortar stores. They sold most of their products through Amazon, and they were selling commodities like fans, sinks, and lights. With customers buying on Amazon, Westside Wholesale needed to somehow create loyalty to their own brand, so they included a coupon for a 10% rebate with every purchase from their website.[48] 10% might sound small, but when I am making a decision, that 10% difference gets me to go to their site and potentially buy from them directly next time. It also means they get to capture an email and begin nurturing the customer for the next sale.

Katie McKeever, a Product Marketing Manager at Yotpo, stresses how crucial loyalty programs can be. She says:

> *"When it comes to loyalty, consumers are increasingly focused on value and convenience. They may pick a brand because it's cheaper or easier to access. Loyalty programs are the key to unlocking long-term retention because they provide the critical value exchange for consumers. Keep your loyalty strategy dynamic, with campaigns that optimize shopping seasons, holidays, and time-sensitive offers. Rewards can include more than just discounts, like VIP experiences. These rewards gamify the buying experience and keep customers excited to come back for more.*
>
> *To maximize the potential of your loyalty program, minimize barriers to entry. Do you require a store account, a minimum spend, etc? It's easy for a loyalty program to be structured in a way where it will only benefit the minority of your customers, and it is not uncommon for loyalty programs to only engage 30% of a brand's customers as a result. While this can be done by design (eg. a VIP club with a min $500 LTV), you can also engage your entire customer base. Customers who earn points through a loyalty program are 3x more likely to make a second purchase. Do you truly need that minimum spend or store account when there is a great deal of earning potential being left on the table?"[49]*

KEY TAKEAWAYS

- In this chapter, we've covered email marketing, SMS, chatbots, content, and loyalty programs. These are all great ways to nurture your community and extend the lifetime value of every customer.

- As you flesh out your nurturing strategy, think of your customers as a community, and think of everyone in that community as a close friend.

- You want to stay in touch and provide value to your friends, right? This might push you to do things we haven't discussed in this chapter, like hosting live events or building a community on social platforms, etc.

- As your relationships with customers deepen, your business becomes more sustainable, defensible, and resistant to unforeseen downturns.

- Loyalty is a moat that keeps your customers close and shields you from conflict, whether it's a competitor, bad press, or even a natural disaster. There are an infinite number of tools to nurture your audience, and they're always changing. But the approach is constant and unwavering.

- Nurture your leads and customers. Stay in touch. Build a relationship.

- The loyalty you earn will naturally lead you to the third and final leg of the marketing tripod: trust.

WANT TO LEARN MORE? Visit www.hawkemethod.com.

ENDNOTES

37. "multitrillion-dollar industry."
How much revenue does email drive? eMarketer. (2015, September 18). From https://www.emarketer.com/Article/How-Much-Revenue-Email-Drive/1013001.

38. "Omnisend."
Sourced from direct interview with Hawke Media Partner, Omnisend, 2021. For more information on Omnisend, see https://www.omnisend.com/.

39. "2019 to 2020."
Omnisend. (2021). *2020 ecommerce STATISTICS Report: Email, SMS & push Messaging insights for 2021.* Omnisend. From https://www.omnisend.com/resources/reports/ecommerce-statistics-report-2021/.

40. "2020 at 51.9%."
Omnisend. (2021). *2020 ecommerce STATISTICS Report: Email, SMS & push Messaging insights for 2021.* Omnisend. From https://www.omnisend.com/resources/reports/ecommerce-statistics-report-2021/.

41. "1.8% of email sends but drove 29%"
Omnisend. (2021). *2020 ecommerce statistics report: Email, SMS & Push Messaging Insights for 2021.* Omnisend. Retrieved October 6, 2021, from https://www.omnisend.com/resources/reports/ecommerce-statistics-report-2021/.

42. "Klaviyo."
Sourced from direct interview with Hawke Media Partner, Klaviyo, 2021. For more information on Klaviyo, see https://www.klaviyo.com/.

43. "a tenfold increase."
Postscript. (2021, August 17). *SMS benchmark REPORT 2021.* Postscript. From https://www.postscript.io/sms-benchmarks/.

44. "ReCharge."

Sourced from direct interview with Hawke Media Partner, ReCharge, 2021. For more information on ReCharge, see https://support.rechargepayments.com/hc/en-us/ sections/1500000617702-RechargeSMS.

45. "Postscript."

Sourced from direct interview with Hawke Media Partner, Postscript, 2021. For more information on Postscript, see https://www.postscript.io/.

46. "Octane AI."

Sourced from direct interview with Hawke Media Partner, Octane AI, 2021. For more information on Octane AI, see https://www.octaneai.com/.

47. "Smile.io."

Sourced from direct interview with Hawke Media Partner, Smile.io, 2021. For more information on Smile.io, see https://smile.io/.

48. "coupon for a 10% rebate"

Cashback in Westside dollars. Westside Wholesale. (2021). From https://www.westsidewholesale.com/rewards-program/.

49. "Yotpo."

Sourced from direct interview with Hawke Media Partner, Yotpo, 2021. For more information on Yotpo see https://www.yotpo.com/.

PART 3

—

Trust

CHAPTER TWELVE

DO YOU TRUST ME?

Trust is the third and final leg of the marketing tripod. This is the last checkbox. Whenever you're building a new marketing campaign or trying to assess an existing marketing campaign, the first step is to analyze each leg of the tripod. It will help you identify your weak points, fix them, and establish a strategy that generates a positive tROI over time.

GIVE ME A COKE AND A BIG MAC

Love it or hate it, when you walk into a McDonald's, you know what you're going to get. Your Big Mac will taste the same whether you're in Connecticut or California or even Moscow (take it from a guy who actually ate a Big Mac in Moscow. It's the same as the Big Mac in LA). McDonald's might change the taste and menu marginally in certain countries to accommodate cultural taste preferences—e.g., John Travolta's line in *Pulp Fiction* about how a Quarter Pounder is called *"a Royale with cheese"* in France—but their supply chain has been so perfected that there's an extremely high level of consistency to their product, which builds trust.

Likewise, if you buy a Coke anywhere in the world—other than swapping corn syrup for sugar in some geographies—nothing else changes in that drink. If you're in another city, state, or country, and you want a Coke, you can trust that it will taste the way you expect it to taste. I'm not debating whether you should like McDonald's or Coke. But from the perspective of trust, these companies are experts.

Studies have shown that 75% of consumers won't purchase from a brand they don't automatically trust.[50] In other words, it's basically a prerequisite to winning an eventual sale. Trust can seem amorphous and hard to measure, but there are ways to do it. And when done right, it acts as a force multiplier. As trust builds, your ads will perform better, and your conversion-to-sale becomes more efficient.

SELLING PRENATAL VITAMINS

When I worked at Science (the startup incubator in LA), one of my first consulting projects was with a vitamin company. They were selling prenatal vitamins to pregnant women through online subscriptions, and they had just launched. There was no press about them. No content. In fact, they were actually white-labeling other vitamins that were totally safe, but they hadn't built any trust for their brand.

If I'm a pregnant woman, I am not going to see a Facebook ad for prenatal pills and say to myself, "Yeah! Their products seem great. I'll buy them right this second." I would need some assurance that the pills were legitimate. This type of purchase requires trust. And this was in 2012 when online purchasing was a lot lower than it is now.

The vitamin company was focusing on Facebook ad optimization and sending emails, but they were doing no press. They asked me what they should do.

"Let's start with the main problem. How do you think you are going to be able to convince a customer to buy this? No one's heard of you. You have no validation. You have no brand. You have to borrow trust from someone else. You have to get third-party validation because, right now, nobody's going to believe in you."

Everyone's been scammed, and you don't want to get scammed buying a pill you're ingesting for your unborn child. Consumer trust in your brand mitigates and eases this concern or risk. So, we decided to implement an influencer strategy. We would borrow trust from others. We found people who were already trusted by the general public, educated them about the product, and got some of them to endorse it and promote it. Borrowing trust isn't wrong. It's what most small companies must do to establish credibility.

There are different levels of trust, depending on what your company sells. If you're selling vitamins to pregnant women, you must establish a high level of trust because there's a monumental risk to the buyer if your product is faulty. The same holds true for airlines and car companies and parachute manufacturers. You get the point. By contrast, if you're selling products in the fashion industry, the level of trust required is lower. In this case, the consumer is worried about the fit and whether or not the item is stylish. Is it going to last? Is it functional?

In the consumer's decision-making process, trust always matters on some level. Understanding the trust factor for your particular product or service will help you gauge how much to invest in this aspect of your business. For Hawke Media, as a marketing agency, trust is a critical factor because we're taking people's money and spending it on their behalf to drive growth for their business. Almost nobody disagrees that they need marketing. Companies understand they need it, which means we need to demonstrate why we are better than the thousands of other competitors in the market.

We achieve that through systematically building trust.

HOW TO BUILD TRUST

I'm building trust with you right now. You are reading my book about how our company thinks about marketing. Although we aren't having a conversation, I'm still communicating with you on a deep level, which builds trust. Publishing this book also gives me credibility, which builds more trust. Finally, we can also use the book as a newsworthy marketing asset. I will do interviews and other press about the book, which builds even more trust. And this book is just one of thousands of pieces of content we put into the world on a consistent basis.

As we build topical authority and credibility, the marketing machine starts to spit out opportunities organically so we don't have to chase them down anymore. But regardless, every new piece of content is leveraged to build trust. We get several press hits a day from experts writing about what we are doing. This happens because those writers trust us. There is no silver bullet to establishing trust, and there is no way to sustain trust without building it with intention over time. Any one ad campaign, one event, one interview is not enough.

Let me give you a few anecdotal examples. During a vacation in Mexico, I wrote this chapter. Even though I was on vacation, I knew the importance of this book and the trust it will build, so I took the time to do it. I also got a call from *Reuters* to be quoted on the political climate as it related to TikTok, a multibillion-dollar company. *Reuters* is a respected publication and TikTok is a highly visible company, so I knew this would lift my credibility through association. Even though I was on vacation, I allocated time to write up a statement so I could be mentioned in the article. I'm not suggesting you always work while you're on vacation. Generally, I try not to do that. But because I understand the value of trust, I make exceptions when I know it will pay dividends later.

Our entire company leverages these opportunities, not just me. We consistently do things to build trust because it's ingrained in our company's culture. There's a reason we seek out awards, and get them. Legitimate awards from respected brands build trust. We throw events to bring people together and talk to us in person. This breaks down the barrier of the two-dimensional screen or a phone call and feels more relational and more human.

The best tool for building trust is consistency. You need consistency in your message, in your product, and in your approach. Day after day, week after week, month after month, year after year. It may save you from bad press or crisis management later on.

The Honest Company had some problems with their products. They were using ingredients that were unhealthy. They had originally reported that these ingredients were not in their products, when in fact, they were.[51] This could have been a game-over moment for The Honest Company, but because they had established such a high level of trust with their audience, most of their customers assumed it was an accident and forgave them. The trust factor can save your business in a case like this.

Without trust, you're just your own cheerleader. People become far less likely to buy from you. This is the third and final leg of the tripod because it's the hardest to measure. But don't ignore it. You *must* build trust to keep your marketing tripod standing tall, because the wind will inevitably howl.

KEY TAKEAWAYS

- Studies have shown that 75% of consumers won't purchase from a brand they don't trust.
- There are different levels of trust, depending on what your company sells.
- If you're in the beginning stages of your company, don't be afraid to leverage third-party validation to borrow trust.
- As you release more content, you'll build topical authority and credibility.
- Trust is difficult to measure, but consistency is key.

WANT TO LEARN MORE? Visit www.hawkemethod.com.

ENDNOTES

50. **"don't automatically trust."**
    Ries, T. E. (2020, June 25). *Trust barometer Special Report: Brand trust in 2020.* Edelman. From https://www.edelman.com/research/brand-trust-2020.

51. **"when in fact they were."**
    Ng, S. (2018, January 5). *No longer a unicorn, Jessica Alba's Honest Co. struggles to grow.* The Wall Street Journal. From https://www.wsj.com/articles/no-longer-a-unicorn-jessica-albas-honest-co-faces-growth-challenges-1515157203.

CHAPTER THIRTEEN

THIRD-PARTY VALIDATION

You can scream as loud as you want about your awesome products, but if people don't know you, it won't matter. Your word means nothing. The way to fix that, in the beginning, is to use third-party validation. You can borrow trust from other people and leverage their audience to build your own. And even when you're a larger company and you've established trust, it still helps to reinforce your brand through third-party validation, so these strategies are never obsolete. Keep them close.

PR AS A DRIVER OF TRUST

As you know, a PR hit generally won't give you much juice in terms of awareness because there's so much content flowing through the internet these days. Unless you catch lightning in a bottle and your press hit goes completely viral, you can't rely on it as a strategy. But PR has other benefits outside of driving awareness.

In today's marketing landscape, PR is best used as an asset for building trust through third-party validation. If *Fast Company* mentions you in an article, they're associating their brand with you. That masthead means something. If you're trying to raise money and *Forbes* has written about you, it means someone at *Forbes* looked at your business and thought it was newsworthy. That's a positive indicator for the investor. And for the general consumer who sees you were featured on *Good Morning America*, it's enough to get them over the edge and trust you.

Once you get that press—and this is where people really miss the boat on PR—you need to share it everywhere. It's an asset that provides immediate validation. Send it in an email to all your potential leads. Put it into your advertisements, add the *Forbes* logo on your website. Link to the article from your site. It's not just about getting the article and having a line in *TechCrunch*. It's about taking that article and showing it off.

Thinking about PR from the perspective of trust will make you value it and understand it better. If you think of it only as a way to drive traffic and awareness, you're missing the bulk of its value and you'll be disappointed. But if you leverage it as a way to control your messaging and build validation and authority, it can be quite powerful.

Controlling the narrative around your company is critical and not just to salvage your reputation should a PR crisis arrive. For Hawke Media, we started positioning ourselves as a marketing consultancy and an outsourced CMO, as opposed to a marketing agency. We got journalists to publish articles about this new innovative model, "The Outsourced CMO," because we didn't want to be seen as *just another* marketing agency. We wanted to distance ourselves from that, and people started to believe we were unique because we had trusted third-party sources validating that narrative.

When I tell a prospective client our team is full of expert-level talent, it's really convenient to be able to back it up with an article about our unique hiring and training process, published in *Entrepreneur*.[52]

It's almost always better for PR to come from someone other than your own company. A statement or announcement can be done through a press release, but frankly, press releases are mostly a waste of time.

As an example, we have a proprietary platform that we're building. At some point, we're going to be able to use it for our clients and it's going to turn into a real powerhouse differentiator for us. At that point, we could do a press release announcing the new platform, but if we can get a trusted third-party publication to talk about it instead, we're building trust.

When COVID-19 went global, it changed the way companies do business. In the midst of the pandemic, we made a swift decision to go fully remote as a company. We could have said nothing about it, or done our own press release. But instead, we put an article in *Ad Age*, which made us look like pioneers because it was deemed newsworthy.[53] It became a viral article in our industry because prior to that, we were known for our large, open-floor headquarters in LA. Getting rid of the office was big news and it was a sign of the times. The third-party validation from posting it on *Ad Age* made it a hot news story. A press release would have gotten lost in the mix.

> **PRO TIP:** Headlines matter. A large percentage of people never read articles, as was the case with Hawke Media's in *Ad Age*. They just read the headline. When crafting an article, read your headline as if it's the only thing the customer sees. If the headline is catchy, great. If it paints you in a positive light, even better. Curiosity is also an important element. The title of our article was, "Three Lessons Learned from Restructuring a Company in a Time of Change." Notice this doesn't sound salesy. It sounds valuable and it evokes curiosity.

TRUST VIA INFLUENCERS

In 2012, I launched an activewear brand called Ellie and we leveraged a thousand influencers. They weren't called influencers at the time. They were just called bloggers. Social media influencers weren't established yet, but blogging was big. We got a thousand bloggers to write reviews on our company. All I had to do was send them $20 of free activewear.

I spent about $20,000 on that campaign and it drove $1.2 million in revenue. Why? Because we figured out how to establish immediate trust. For twenty bucks a pop, I had to know each blogger would drive at least one sale to break even. We were targeting the top bloggers in fashion, so they had relatively large audiences. Forecasting just one sale per article was conservative, so we went full scale with it. If my favorite fitness blogger tells me they love this activewear, I'm going to trust them.

There are multiple benefits to this approach because we borrowed trust from the bloggers, but we also borrowed their audiences. The whole process had nothing to do with our brand. And yet we were able to push $1.2 million in product with a $20,000 spend. We could have run ads all day on Facebook, but without any third-party validation, our campaigns would have tanked.

The influencer marketing space shifted significantly after the Fyre Festival disaster.[54] If you're not familiar with the story, Fyre Festival was hyped up to be the best music festival in history. The company ran a huge influencer campaign where top influencers posted a blank orange square on their Instagram and other social media accounts at the same time. The mystery of the orange square created a buzz with media outlets and eventually the news came out about the festival. The marketing material and website showed a tropical paradise, high-end bungalows on the beach, and an incredible lineup of musicians.

Unfortunately, the whole thing was a hoax. They didn't actually have the budget to run the event. People booked their flights and got to the location, only to realize there was no festival. The company had run out of money and overpromised on something they couldn't possibly deliver.

People were furious at the influencers, but it wasn't really their fault. They didn't know the details of what they were promoting. Everybody lost in this situation. The influencers looked bad, the company failed, and the customers were livid. Influencer campaigns had become a commoditized form of advertising by 2012, but it was causing influencers to lose credibility with their audiences. Fyre Festival was the nail in the coffin.

After the Fyre Festival disaster, the FTC realized they had to crack down on this type of marketing.[55] Now influencers must disclose if they're promoting a brand, which takes the entire trust piece out of it. So influencer marketing went from being a powerful audience and trust builder to just another ad channel. An influencer posting about our company on Instagram is now essentially the same as me just running an ad on Instagram.

It's still similar to a micro-endorsement and you can get some awareness from it, but it's not scalable and never has been. We recommend keeping it as a small part of the marketing mix, but it's not a driving force like it was in its glory days.

While influencer marketing is not our preferred method, influencers can drive some top-of-funnel awareness. Cohley, a content engineering platform that frequently works with influencers, sees the upside that user-generated content can have for brands, especially as marketers move towards crafting authentic, one-on-one relationships with increasingly discerning consumers. Cohley Co-founder and CEO, Tom Logan, said:

> *"Influencers provide the most value when they're leveraged as the talented content creators they are. They are highly adept at creating authentic, branded content that can drive*

performance in ads, organic social, emails, and websites. Influencer-generated content helps brands meet today's enormous content demands and provides them with the inputs they need to power sophisticated testing strategies."[56]

ENDORSEMENT DEALS

There's a blurred line for what constitutes a true endorsement deal. For the purposes of this book, we're talking about ubiquitous or well-known celebrities, even if they started as influencers. A "household name," like Brad Pitt, Lebron James, Tony Robbins, or Kim Kardashian.

This is a shortcut to creating your brand identity because it immediately tells your audience who you are. The celebrity becomes part of your brand by association. If you partner with the right celebrity, it can work incredibly well. This is all about aspiration. Who do your customers want to be like?

Do you remember the iconic Michael Jordan jingle by Gatorade? "I want to be like Mike."[57]

It was a brilliant campaign. The message is, "If I buy this product, I become Michael Jordan." Who doesn't want to be Michael Jordan? Gatorade built trust with third-party validation, while also capturing their brand identity in a single commercial.

Remember how The Honest Company skated through a potential PR disaster that I spoke about in Chapter 12? Jessica Alba was their celebrity endorser. She's the young, beautiful mom from California who wants her kids to be healthy and safe. Her personal brand fit well with The Honest Company, so they leveraged it and partnered with her. And it helped save them.

Endorsements can go wrong when the endorser doesn't match the product. Imagine a bottom-shelf vodka brand doing an endorsement deal with a popular rapper. While he's endorsing the bottom-shelf vodka on television, he's drinking top-shelf vodka at the club—and people notice things like that. The campaign then seems disingenuous; it's obviously just a ploy to get people to buy your product because the rapper is cool. It's a bad alignment. The celebrity has to actually like the product and use it, especially today when everyone has a camera in their pocket.

My favorite example of this is Ryan Reynolds with Aviation Gin and Mint Mobile. He invested his own money into both companies and started a marketing agency to do all the creative for their ad campaigns. He helps write the ad copy. He loves this stuff. As you might expect, both companies are crushing it. Reynolds even jokingly said Aviation Gin would get a product placement in every movie he's in. Part of the contract.[58]

He's a goofy guy. He's a good-looking guy. Charismatic. He's got a happy marriage and kids. He's the fun, young dad living his life and having a good time. People are simple, psychologically. They see Ryan drinking this gin all the time, and subconsciously, they're thinking, "I can be a good-looking, classy, funny guy if I drink this gin. I can be just like Ryan Reynolds."

> **PRO TIP:** If you can get your celebrity endorser to invest directly in the company, you align incentives and will typically see a much better, more sustainable result.

These deals aren't easy to do. When a deal happens, most of the time the celebrity and the people on their team want upfront cash. And the celebrity often doesn't want to take the risk of cutting a seven-figure check on an unproven startup. While it may be tough, if you can find a celebrity who believes in what you're doing and can invest their time and money, it's the most powerful endorsement you can get.

PARTNERSHIPS

Partnerships are significantly underrated. They have been our #1 driver for success at Hawke Media. The nuance of partnerships is in finding other companies who share your audience but are non-competitive. Then you can lend trust and awareness to each other. At Hawke Media, we're partnered with all sorts of other boutique marketing agencies, design shops, email marketing software companies, and other complementary companies. When they hear a customer needs marketing help, they send them to us. When we hear a customer needs email software, we send them to our partner. This works for B2B and B2C companies.

Partnerships are lucrative because, oftentimes, the partner refers one of their paying customers over to you. The customer needs the partner's service, but they also need your service. Since they're already paying the partner, and the partner is recommending you, the customer already has a much higher propensity to buy than a cold lead. And you pass your customers to them in the same way.

This is a situation where one plus one equals four, because now we can blend our audiences to increase sales on both sides. It costs nothing other than a little time. Relationship management doesn't have to be complicated. For example, gifting between partners has worked well for us. Giftagram, Loop & Tie, and Giftology are all good companies that facilitate corporate gifting if you need a place to start.

You can do cross-promotions in many different ways, whether it's just referring business back and forth, cross-promotional email blasts, hosting events together, or other promotional activity.

If you're a B2C company, this could be a "Gift with Purchase" for each other, cross-selling on each other's websites, or even launching ad campaigns that cross-promote. AT&T does it with Apple all the time. They love promoting Apple because it's a positive brand association.

In cases like these, both companies will throw in money for campaigns. They get to split the costs and both brands get visibility to the same number of people. Mutual trust is being built on both sides. AT&T customers now also trust Apple a little more, and vice versa.

> **PRO TIP:** Find smart, time-efficient ways to collaborate. DojoMojo is a clever company that pairs six-to-ten companies that have similar-sized email lists and audiences. They all do a promotion together to the combined list. As a result, you're all sharing this pool of audience with nearly 10x your own email list for the promo, without any hard cost.

REVIEWS & TESTIMONIALS

Testimonials probably won't be a massive driver of success, but having some case studies or people talking about your product is always helpful in building trust. If I'm trying to decide whether or not I should buy a product, I might want to hear from another actual customer. This is third-party validation from someone who has actually purchased and used the thing I'm about to buy. A study from BrightLocal highlights the importance of reviews: 88% of people seek them out before visiting a business.[59]

Testimonials on a third-party site like Amazon can also help, because people know you can't doctor those, versus just hosting them on your own site. Our partners at Trustpilot, another third-party review site, stress the importance of consumer reviews.

"Engaging with every customer review, both positive and negative, as it is one of the most effective strategies to managing your brand reputation. Responding to each

review can help businesses win back frustrated customers and turn those negative reviews into positive experiences. It also shows that the brand really cares what their customers think of them!"[60]

There are a nearly infinite number of ways to gain third-party validation. These are just a few of them. In the next chapter, we'll talk about how to build more trust through the brand itself.

KEY TAKEAWAYS

- You can borrow trust from other people and leverage their audience to build your own.
- In today's marketing landscape, PR is best used as an asset for building trust through third-party validation.
- Controlling the narrative around your company is another way to use PR to build trust and negate naysayers.
- When crafting an article, read your headline as if it's the only thing the customer sees.
- Endorsements, testimonials, and partnerships can also build positive third-party validation when done correctly.

WANT TO LEARN MORE? Visit www.hawkemethod.com.

ENDNOTES

52. "published in _Entrepreneur._"

Delmercado, T. (2018, March 7). Don't lose those talented team Members. 3 ways to hold on to them. Entrepreneur. From https://www.entrepreneur.com/article/309956.

53. "was deemed newsworthy."

Huberman, E. (2020, July 21). _Three lessons learned from restructuring a company in a time of change._ Ad Age. From https://adage.com/article/industry-insights/three-lessons-learned-restructuring-company-time-change/2268991.

54. "Fyre Festival disaster."

Coscarelli, J., & Ryzik, M. (2017, April 28). _Fyre festival, a Luxury Music Weekend, crumbles in the Bahamas._ The New York Times. From https://www.nytimes.com/2017/04/28/arts/music/fyre-festival-ja-rule-bahamas.html.

55. "this type of marketing."

Disclosures 101 for social media influencers. Federal Trade Commission. (2019, November 7). From https://www.ftc.gov/tips-advice/business-center/guidance/disclosures-101-social-media-influencers.

56. "Cohley."

Sourced from direct interview with Hawke Media Partner, Cohley, 2021. For more information on Cohley, see https://www.cohley.com/.

57. "I want to be like Mike."

Rovell, D. (2016, August 8). _Famed 'be Like mike' Gatorade Ad Debuted 25 years ago._ ESPN. From https://www.espn.com/nba/story/_/id/17246999/michael-jordan-famous-mike-gatorade-commercial-debuted-25-years-ago-monday.

58. "Aviation Gin."

Al-Ghamdi, A. (2020, July 25). _Ryan Reynolds Adds A Stealthy Gin Ad Into A Scene From His Buried Movie._ ScreenRant. From https://screenrant.com/ryan-reynolds-buried-movie-scene-aviation-gin-edit-video/.

59. "BrightLocal."

Marchant, R. (2014, December 12). Local consumer Review SURVEY 2014. BrightLocal. Retrieved September 24, 2021, from https://www.brightlocal.com/research/local-consumer-review-survey-2014/?_ga=2.102443011.384987211.1624213117-1049392863.1621956785.

60. "Trustpilot."

Sourced from direct interview with Hawke Media Partner, Trustpilot, 2021. For more information on Trustpilot, see https://www.trustpilot.com/.

CHAPTER FOURTEEN

BRAND

We've all seen the golden arches. Just Do It. The apple with a bite taken out of it. Even without telling you the brand, you know it. Those brands bring with them a certain emotional appeal, or a certain distaste for you. They are linked to specific memories or moods. There's a consistent feeling you get from that brand, good or bad. The name, the logo, the slogan, the product, the company itself—what kind of emotions are called up for you?

Brand is synonymous with trust. If your brand is consistent, you won't need as much third-party validation, so everything becomes a little easier. It's easier to reach new customers through word-of-mouth, easier to convert them into buyers, and easier to cultivate a deeper relationship with them over time to extend LTV. Your brand also flows into everything your company touches, from your customer service, to your marketing, and even your packaging.

CONSISTENCY IN YOUR BUSINESS

Whatever you do consistently and repetitively is your brand. It becomes your personality, your aura, your reputation.

What are you known for and why?

If you're training for a marathon and I gave you the option of using a random running shoe from a no-name brand, or a pair of Nike running shoes, which would you choose? The vast majority of us would go with Nike. We gravitate toward Nike because we *know* Nike. We know it's tried and true and they've been making sneakers for over forty years. Nike is a brand that comes with an expected level of reliability and quality.

On the flipside of the coin, you can end up with a bad reputation if you aren't careful. Uber became known for bullying, well, because they consistently bullied their employees, their partners, their competitors, and their drivers.[61] That became their brand, and they've had to try to combat that reputation ever since.

Your behavior becomes your culture, and this is where your brand is formed. What do you emphasize? What is your mission? How do you manage your people? If you emphasize quality and you consistently deliver quality products, your brand will become synonymous with quality. At Hawke, we've consistently made it easy to work with us. We've built ease of use, friendliness, and inclusiveness into our brand ethos. Companies like to write down core values. But you can't just write them down. The behavior must back them up.

Take for example, Arka, a leading provider in eco-friendly and sustainable packaging.[62] They've helped thousands of brick-and-mortar stores go online and create an omnichannel presence. Their core values don't end at their customer-facing activities, though. They back it up. As a company, they are FSC Certified by the Forestry Services for the Chain of Custody standard of sustainably sourced materials. Their facilities are aligned with sustainable practices. They have ISO certification and offer carbon-neutral shipping by offsetting emissions. This is a company that truly lives their brand.

YOUR LOGO IS NOT YOUR BRAND

People tend to think "brand" is a color scheme and a logo, but in fact, your brand is whatever that color scheme and logo represent. Your logo is a visual symbol that triggers the feelings and associations created by your company, which is formed through your actions over time.

Every person ties a unique association to a brand. When I see the golden arches, I can taste a Big Mac. McDonald's achieved that through consistency. That exact taste has been stored in my long-term memory. They've trained my brain over many years to call up that specific taste whenever I see the unique visual image of the golden arches.

It sounds creepy, but it's not. It's just McDonald's doing what they do on a consistent basis and building that relationship over time. It's the same reaction that happens when you see a loved one; your brain calls up the associations with that person and produces a specific feeling. Likewise, the logo and brand colors are simply the visual representation of the company.

MAKE A MARKETING PERSONA

Mapping your company to a specific person is an effective way to define your brand. The idea is to create a fictional person who would be the ideal representation of the company's brand. If you can find an actual person or a celebrity who matches the brand, that's even better. This is an obvious endorsement opportunity, but even if you don't partner with the celebrity, you can use them as your avatar when making business decisions to stay on brand.

When I started my activewear brand, Ellie, we created a twenty-seven-year-old woman named Amy from California as our marketing persona. For every email, article, social media post, product decision, partnership, we would ask ourselves, "Would Amy be into this? Is this something Amy would do?"

We got deeper and deeper into who Amy was and what motivated her. What were her aspirations? This makes it much easier to figure out nuances in your marketing strategy, like writing copy or designing creative for ad campaigns. Amy isn't too serious, so we made our content more casual. Amy loves the outdoors, so we would use images of beautiful places around the world in our creatives—places Amy would want to visit. It might seem funny to be so specific with your marketing persona, but the more specific you can get, the better. It helps you create marketing that feels targeted and genuine.

Lululemon's founder, Chip Wilson, has talked about their marketing persona, a thirty-two-year-old woman.[63] Not thirty-three. Not thirty-one.

We were equally specific when envisioning Amy's character. Amy has big aspirations, a long road ahead of her, and feels she has enough time to conquer those goals in her future, while exploring her interests. She has a younger sister, so she enjoys providing guidance as a mentor, but still feels there is room to grow into herself as a role model. With this type of character development, our marketing spoke to a very specific person, but we still attracted people from a range of ages and life stages. And that worked.

For Hawke Media, the brand is me as the founder. There's an ego trap there, but I had to get over it and realize it was an accurate portrayal of our brand, and using me as the avatar would help us remain true to our values. We do goofy stuff like I do in my everyday life. We have fun with things. It doesn't necessarily fit the narrative of a marketing consultancy, but it fits our company personality and it makes us more unique. We're not a suit-wearing, serious company. We prefer a more laid-back, light-hearted culture, and we think that helps us create better marketing campaigns. It allows our team to stay creative, take chances, and share ideas. It also helped us identify and attract our ideal customers.

YOUR AVATAR IS NOT YOUR CUSTOMER

Your avatar is not your actual customer, it's who your customer aspires to be. Your target customer and the subject of your messaging are necessarily distinct. Who you're targeting and what your messaging looks like are very different.

A stark (even somewhat unsettling) example of this is ShoeDazzle, a huge e-commerce company. Kim Kardashian was the face of the company, and who she represented was every bit of their branding. At the time, Kim Kardashian was in her twenties, seen as a fashionista, and a city girl. And yet, ShoeDazzle's biggest customer segment was black women in their late forties, living primarily in the rural South. This sounds like a paradox, and it is. But for whatever reason, that demographic gravitated toward that aspiration. This is just the data.

But it clearly demonstrates that your avatar is not your customer.

THE POWER OF SYMBOLS

If you hear brand names like Apple or Coca-Cola, you immediately see their logos in your head. These symbols have become iconic. The best logos are almost like religious symbols. In fact, the Holy Cross is probably one of the most recognized brands in the world. Entire cathedrals are designed around it. People regularly get a tattoo of the Star of David (which is hilarious to me because as someone growing up in Judaism, we were taught not to get tattoos!).

Whenever we are designing a logo, simplicity is a big part of it. It must be unique and iconic so people can remember it, repeat it, and recognize it—just like a religious symbol.

Facebook's logo is just the Facebook Blue brand color and their famous "f." This works because it's unique, easy to visualize, and they put it everywhere. Anytime you have an experience with that brand, you're going to have an interaction with their symbol. Over time, as your customers build relationships with the brand, that symbol becomes increasingly powerful.

Motorcyclists get the Harley Davidson logo tattooed on their bodies because they feel so emotionally aligned with the brand that it becomes a religious symbol for them, just like the Star of David or the Holy Cross. This is how you become a cult brand and a brand that stands for more than just the products you sell. You become an emotion, an ethos, a feeling, a way of life.

BRAND AS AN INTERNAL MOTIVATOR

Your brand's symbol is more important for your internal team than it is for your customers in the early days. This gets back to culture. Your external brand comes from your internal cultural brand. Will the logo attract the type of team members you want? Can people on the team rally behind it? Will they want to fly it on a flag outside their house? Should it be old-fashioned or futuristic? Rigid or flowy?

Where I grew up in Ojai, California, there's a lot of wilderness and wildlife, and I loved going into the mountains to look for red-tailed hawks. One particular day as a six-year-old, I was told that my spirit animal was a hawk. That stuck with me.

I've started many companies, but with this one, I wanted it to come from me. It was personal. Our logo is red for the red-tailed hawk, with a simple shape of a hawk landing on top of the words. I felt good about putting my time and effort into it. There was meaning and pride in it.

More practically speaking, there are some beneficial aspects to the name. I didn't know any other well-known business brands that used the hawk as a symbol or wordmark, and it's a strong animal. Without much competition in the market, I thought we could own the hawk as a visual icon. We now officially own the trademark for "Hawke."

We added the "e" because I searched for the domain with regular spelling and it was taken. But adding the "e" has worked in our favor. It would have been harder to trademark the name "Hawk" because it isn't unique. The "e" also has some subtle meanings. "e" for Erik. "E" for e-commerce and e-marketing. It's all part of our brand story. Adding the "e" helped us rank more easily in SEO for the specific search term "Hawke" with an "e."

As we built up our awareness, people began searching for us directly with the unique spelling, which led to more people finding it. Eventually, Google recognized that when people type "Hawk Media," they actually want "Hawke Media," so we still show up. As we got bigger, we were in a position to buy the domain without the "e" from the original owner. We still keep the "e," but now we can direct all of the traffic from hawkmedia.com to our actual site, hawkemedia.com.

Sometimes people get too caught up in naming their company. Look at some of the biggest brands in the world, including Google. A googol is a number. It's a 1 with one hundred zeros after it. Google's mission is to organize the world's information, which seems infinite and impossible, just like a googol. It also only has the numbers 1 and 0 which is the basis of binary code.

The brand name can simply be something meaningful for the founders and early employees. Later, your reputation starts to form around the name, associations, and iconography.

THE FREE WAY TO IMPROVE YOUR MARKETING FOR THE NEXT ONE HUNDRED YEARS

Outside of getting your logo designed and your brand colors figured out, building your brand doesn't cost a penny. It just requires deliberate attention. You should always be focused on this. It's no surprise that our most successful clients treat their brand as a critical piece of their strategy. It is arguably the most important element of any marketing approach for sustained, long-term success, and it's almost always the most underappreciated aspect of marketing because people don't understand what it is or how to define it.

If your company is going to be around one-hundred years from now, it won't be because you were good at running ads or you had a good conversion rate. It will be because your brand is so strong that it's passed down from generation to generation. That's true customer loyalty at its best.

Amazon doesn't need to market anymore. They've created a brand of quick delivery, reliability, ease of use, and access to everything. Most products on Amazon are also available on the original manufacturer's website for a cheaper price, but customers buy from Amazon because they know the Amazon brand. They know the item will be delivered quickly and reliably, that returns are easy, and that the payment and shipping information is already stored for maximum ease-of-use. They're nearly bulletproof.

KEY TAKEAWAYS

- If your brand is consistent, you won't need as much third-party validation, so everything becomes a little easier.
- Whatever you do consistently and repetitively is your brand.
- People think "brand" is a color scheme and a logo, but your brand is whatever that color scheme and logo represents.
- Mapping your company to a specific person is an effective way to define your brand.
- The best logos are almost like religious symbols. Simple and iconic.

WANT TO LEARN MORE? Visit www.hawkemethod.com.

ENDNOTES

61. "Uber."

Siddiqui, F., & Albergotti, R. (2020, October 22). *Uber drivers sue app over 'constant barrage' PUSHING CALIFORNIA anti-employment initiative.* The Washington Post. From https://www.washingtonpost.com/technology/2020/10/22/uber-prop22-suit/.

62. "Arka."

Sourced from direct interview with Hawke Media Partner, Arka, 2021. For more information on Arka, see https://www.arka.com/.

63. "thirty-two-year-old woman."

Lutz, A. (2015, February 2). *Lululemon calls its ideal Customers 'OCEAN' AND 'duke' - here's everything we know about them.* Yahoo! Finance. From https://finance.yahoo.com/news/lululemon-calls-ideal-customers-ocean-211842519.html.

CHAPTER FIFTEEN

THE FUTURE OF MARKETING

Before we talk about the future of marketing, let's talk about the history. Advertising began around 35 C.E. in the form of signs outside of shops. That's storefront advertising. Around 1450, flyers and brochures were given out to attract passers-by. Print advertising began around 1600, which is the first-known form of paid advertising. The first billboards appeared around 1867. Radio ads debuted around 1920, then television ads in 1941, telemarketing in 1950, database marketing in the 1980s, digital marketing in 1993, and finally social media, content marketing, and influencer marketing into the 2000s.[64]

We're living in a time when you can target anybody you want. You can reach any audience, but most marketing is still managed manually. Existing software typically only works well for one-to-many communication, so it isn't very personalized. The ability to automate and customize is elementary. Machine learning is making a lot of progress, but it's not replacing marketers—yet. We are tracking everything. The data is there. The computing power and A.I. technology just needs to catch up.

See the image below on how far marketing has come.

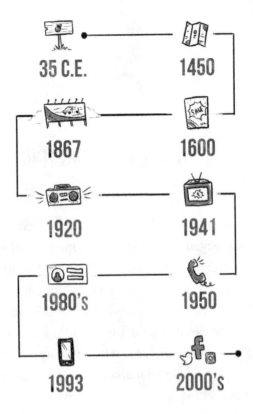

There's plenty of controversy around how companies are tracking data, but as a marketer, it's a positive to be able to identify and target almost anybody. As a millennial and a consumer, I'm honestly okay with data collection. If you're using it to manipulate me in a way that's nefarious, that's when it becomes a problem. But if you're using it to show me a fashion brand I might like because you know my interests, great. That just makes it easier for me to find cool things and easier for the company to reach me.

The problem with the Cambridge Analytica scandal wasn't the targeting part of it or the data part of it.[65] To me, the real problem was how the data was leveraged. That's where we need control and regulation. It's scary because social media algorithms can create echo chambers, meaning I only see one side of the story because it's what Facebook thinks I want to see. That part of the algorithm is bad, but I think they're working on fixing it.

PROGRAMMATIC MARKETING

Programmatic marketing uses machine-learning and A.I. technology to optimize your ad campaigns and complete tasks faster than a human can. For example, it can automatically analyze the click-through rates for thousands of different ad copy and image variations, determine the highest-performing combination, and then display the best ad and trash the others.

It sounds great, but the technology isn't good enough yet to outdo a human—at least not in all aspects of marketing. And frankly, the computation speed isn't fast enough either.

According to American inventor and futurist, Ray Kurzweil, in 2017 computers had the processing ability of a mouse brain. In 2018, the memory capacity of computers surpassed that of humans. A computer can hold more data than the human brain, but the processing power still lags behind. Kurzweil believes computer power will surpass human-brain processing power around 2023.[66] At the time of this writing, computers are somewhere between a mouse brain and a human brain when we consider both memory and processing power together.

Conservatively speaking, we have roughly another decade or so before computers can replace human thinking beyond rudimentary logic. Optimizing your marketing solely with machine learning and A.I. probably won't give you the best results.

We're close. But we're not there yet. Keep an eye out.

WILL A.I. MAKE MARKETERS OBSOLETE?

The first jobs that will get (or have already gotten) replaced by A.I. are blue-collar jobs. McDonald's is already replacing their cashiers with kiosks. Warehouses and factories are replacing their workers with robots. These jobs are easily replicated by computers because they're repetitive, predictable, and logic-driven. That's easy for a computer to learn. However, computers have started encroaching on white-collar jobs too. Lawyers, accountants, and even general-practitioner doctors may soon be replaced with machines. What does this leave? The last jobs remaining will be creative in nature. Computers will likely handle these jobs, too, eventually—but not for a long time.

Let's investigate an example to determine the current state of A.I.'s potential in the marketing landscape. Say Nike is doing some ad campaigns and they're testing two different ads. One ad features a picture of a middle-aged woman running. Another ad says "40% Off Today Only" in big letters. Which ad is going to get more sales? Obviously, the discount ad is going to convert more direct sales. In this case, the computer will tell you that the discount advertisement is the better performing ad. It's going to run a ton of those ads and stop running the other ad. With our current technology capabilities, the computer can't understand all the nuances of the ads. It's only looking at conversion to direct sale. It can't measure the lifetime value of your consumers, or what will build more trust in your brand.

So the A.I. decides that the discount ad is converting well, but it ignores the fact that it's cutting into your profit margins. Is that sustainable? It can't decipher the purchasers likely are price-conscious consumers, nevermind that it doesn't speak to the company's brand avatar whatsoever. Is that what you want?

The other ad of the middle-aged woman running allows Nike to keep 100% of the revenue generated since there is no discount offered.

They're also speaking to a specific audience and building a long-term relationship with a better, more targeted customer. The computer can't possibly understand these nuances. Not yet.

What does the future hold? Highly-targeted, multi-contextual and behavioral marketing. Google and Facebook are installed on my computer and my phone. I'm logged in all the time. The phone companies know my location. These companies are watching my purchase behavior and my activities. With enough data, marketers can serve incredibly targeted ads at the perfect time.

Let's say the data juggernauts know I haven't bought a rain jacket in five years. They also know my travel schedule because I booked my flight online. I'm going to Portland, OR and I live in Santa Monica, CA, where it is sunny all the time. They know the forecast by querying more data, and they can see it will be raining in Portland during my trip. The day before my trip, they send an ad to my phone:

> "We see you're going to Portland. Did you know it's going to be raining the whole week? You live in Santa Monica, so we thought you might need a raincoat. We found a great raincoat from Columbia, a brand you've purchased from before. We can have it delivered to your hotel, the Marriott in downtown Portland, by the time you arrive. Would you like us to make this purchase with your card on file ending in 9834 and set up the delivery?"

Yes! Columbia gets a sale. You get a product you need from a brand you trust, with an extremely high level of convenience and ease of use. The data companies get a cut of the sale. Everybody wins. This type of experience is coming soon, which is why I'm a proponent of data. When leveraged properly, it improves the customer experience.

AVOID SHINY OBJECTS AND DON'T BE A GUINEA PIG

When Google Glass ran a test launch, I was one of their beta users. I also beta tested the Oculus Rift. Everyone was talking about how AR and VR would be the next big thing in marketing, but after testing these products from A-list companies, I knew we had some time before the technology would gain mass adoption. The products just weren't ready.

It's fun to be innovative, but chasing the "shiny object" in marketing is dangerous because there's no benefit to being the first mover. Unless you can get a ton of press or you have some insider knowledge that gives you an edge, you're better off waiting. There are so many kinks in these platforms that it's typically not a benefit in marketing to being the first mover.

The first-mover advantage is a fallacy in marketing and it's a fallacy in business. It's a short-sighted viewpoint. The first mover in social networking wasn't Facebook, or even MySpace. It was Friendster.[67] The first mover in search wasn't Google, it was a company called AltaVista.[68] This concept holds true for marketing, too.

Let other people make the mistakes. Let them figure out how to use the platform. Once it stabilizes and matures, you can fold it into your strategy and maximize it. Just don't be the guinea pig.

Billboards have been around since 1867 and are still a great advertising channel.[69] Paid advertising has been around for over 400 years. Still works great. Don't worry about being hyper-innovative with your entire marketing strategy. It's more important to figure out what works well for your brand specifically.

That said, keep your ear to the ground. Sometimes interesting opportunities arise. I believe that TikTok, as it grows through its nascence, will become a powerful advertising platform. Time will tell. As a general rule, 10-20% of your marketing budget should be spent on new channels and new strategies because your current strategies will lose efficacy over time. That's just the way it works. The market is always moving and changing. Some existing channels will saturate, while some will burn out altogether.

I can make one claim about the future of marketing with confidence. Your marketing tripod will have three legs. Those legs will be *awareness, nurturing,* and *trust.* And if you build your marketing strategy with that tripod in mind, your brand will compete, grow, and thrive.

ENDNOTES

64. "marketing into the 2000s."
Out of Home Advertising Association of America, INC. (n.d.).
History of OOH. Out of Home Advertising Association of
America, INC. From https://oaaa.org/AboutOOH/OOHBasics/
HistoryofOOH.aspx.

65. "Cambridge Analytica."
Seetharaman, D., & Bindley, K. (2018, March 23). *Facebook
controversy: What to know About Cambridge Analytica and
your data.* The Wall Street Journal. Retrieved September
24, 2021, from https://www.wsj.com/articles/facebook-
scandal-what-to-know-about-cambridge-analytica-and-your-
data-1521806400.

66. "processing power around 2023"
Kurzweil, R. (2003, March 2). *THE HUMAN MACHINE
MERGER: ARE WE HEADED FOR THE MATRIX?* Kurzweil
Tracking the acceleration of intelligence. From https://www.
kurzweilai.net/the-human-machine-merger-are-we-headed-for-
the-matrix.

67. "Friendster."
Ulunma. (2020, March 21). *Before Facebook there was...
Friendster? Yes, That's right!* Digital Innovation and
Transformation. From https://digital.hbs.edu/platform-digit/
submission/before-facebook-there-was-friendster-yes-thats-
right/.

68. "AltaVista."
Smith, E. (2021, January 4). *Whatever Happened to AltaVista,
Our First Good Search Engine.* VICE. From https://www.vice.
com/en/article/y3gn5v/whatever-happened-to-altavista-our-first-
good-search-engine&sa=D&source=editors&ust=1632267284724
000&usg=AOvVaw1GHS2UKG5aAW5KRrhJAPCG.

69. "great advertising channel."
Refer to source in note 64.

WANT TO LEARN MORE?

The Hawke Method isn't just a book.
It's a way of doing business.

If you want to supercharge your experience,
please join us online at:
www.hawkemethod.com

ABOUT THE AUTHOR

Erik Huberman is the founder and CEO of Hawke Media, the fastest growing marketing consultancy in the United States. Launched in 2014, Hawke Media has grown to over 250 employees. The company has serviced over 3,000 brands of all sizes, ranging from startups to household names.

Prior to Hawke, Huberman founded and sold two successful e-commerce companies. As a serial entrepreneur and marketing expert, Huberman is a sought-after thought leader in the world of digital marketing, entrepreneurship, sales, and business.

Huberman is a frequent contributor to top-tier outlets, a public speaker, and also the recipient of numerous honors and awards, including *Forbes "30Under30," CSQ "40Under40," Inc. "Top 25 Marketing Influencers,"* and *Best in Biz North America "Marketing Executive of the Year."* He is a lifelong believer in giving back to the community and sits on multiple boards. He lives with his wife and dog in Santa Monica, California, where Hawke Media is headquartered.

GLOSSARY

Affiliate

An affiliate, in general business terms, is an "official attachment" of one business entity to another. But informal partnerships of companies in the same industry are becoming more common. Think about it as a codependent or mutually beneficial relationship. Slightly different than a *partner*, since affiliates generally stand to gain a direct percentage of sales from referrals.

The Abandoned Cart

A method to nurture your customers and motivate them to complete a purchase. They've put an item in their online shopping cart, but didn't officially order. So, you send the customer an automated email or text message that reminds them and offers to help if needed.

Average Order Value

Take into consideration the pricing of all your products or services. When a customer makes a purchase, what's the mathematical average of their purchase price? There's your AOV. It's important to note that the higher your AOV, the longer your *Consideration Periods* and *Purchase Cycles* tend to be.

B2B

An acronym for "Business to Business." A B2B company sells products or services to other businesses, rather than consumers. Think software or ergonomics solutions behind the scenes. Hawke Media generally functions as a B2B organization in that we help other businesses market to their own audiences directly rather than selling products to individual consumers.

B2C

An acronym for "Business to Consumer." Some people call it, "Direct to Consumer," abbreviated DTC. It's the same thing. B2C companies are what they sound like. Companies who sell products or services directly to individual purchasers. Retail companies qualify under the business-to-consumer umbrella. Note that *B2B* and B2C qualifications are not mutually exclusive. Many companies have products for both, like Google and Microsoft.

Banner Websites

Underdeveloped websites only containing company info, a baseline description of the product, members of the team, and a contact form. Your company shows up on Google, but there's no method for customers to buy. This hurts *Conversions*.

Blue Chip Companies

This is an old-school term, for old-school companies. They've been around for decades, have been publicly traded for decades, and can boast a history of brand awareness. You might even call them "the old guard" of their respective industries. They've set the tone of what consumers want, and aren't likely going away without some catastrophic PR blunder. And most still won't.

Bootstrap

The term makes us recall "The American Dream." Essentially it means launching a successful enterprise with little capital or money. One of the first appearances of the term was in James Joyce's *Ulysses*. It was first used sarcastically to mean "an impossible endeavor" but has graduated to be a call-to-arms for entrepreneurs.

Bounce Rate

A measured frequency that tells how often a customer visits a site, but leaves immediately. Your bounce rate is a metric detailing missed *Conversions* or information collection. You want it low. High bounce rates can come from a litany of reasons: poor design, confusing content, long load times, links that don't work, etc.

Brand Identity v. "Brand"

Your brand is more than your logo or design. It's what customers associate with your company that's then translated into the color schemes, images, and text of your logo.

C-suite

C-Suite informally refers to the executive team at a company. The top dogs like CEO, COO, *CMO*, any title that contains the word, "Chief."

CAC

An acronym for "Cost to Acquire a Customer." It's an equation that measures the cost of a marketing/ad campaign against the number of new customers brought in and how much they're paying for a service or product. In other words, how much did you spend on that campaign, or, how many new customers did it bring in, and how much did they spend?

Cannibalize

A market situation in which a new product/service from a brand directly competes with an older or outside product/service, jeopardizing their current consumer base. For example, when you give Amazon permission to list your product on their site, they also drive new/old traffic to competitors with similar products. Hence, eating some of your own customer base hoping it drives new customers.

Clickthrough Rate

A base-level marketing datapoint that measures how many clicks your links or advertisements get. What percentage of viewers clicked on the ad? This statistic can be applied to an *Impression*, email *Open Rates*, links directly in your email marketing, or online advertisements, among countless others.

Chatbot

Using software to communicate online with consumers in lieu of a real, live human. Chatbots can automate conversations, interact on messaging platforms, and answer a multitude of questions if programmed correctly. Saves manpower, but can risk alienating new customers if the execution feels robotic and inauthentic.

CMO

An acronym for, "Chief Marketing Officer."

Cohort

Industry term for groups of customers. You can group folks in countless ways, but a useful one is to group cohorts by when they last bought. This way, you can track their engagement and purchase histories over time—to divide the cohorts even further—which stands to make your *Retargeting* efforts stronger.

Consideration Period

The period between a customer initially seeing an advertisement and when they make their first purchase. See *Purchase Cycle* for more.

Content Marketing

Content marketing is like soft advertising. A business will inject demand within their existing audience by providing value through experiences or digital content that's not directly linked to their product or services. Writing an article on a trend in your industry is a common example of content marketing.

Conversion Rate	A conversion rate is an equation that online advertisers and marketers use to compare the total number of visitors to a website to the number that become paying customers, subscribers, or users. It's used to see how good your copy is, how successful and fluid your media are, and how clear your message is, among other things.
Conversion Funnel	How you nurture your customers after they've become part of your audience or engaged with an advertisement. It's the methods and outreach that converts awareness into sales. In other words, the ways you take a prospect and lock in a sale.
Cookies	Tracking codes embedded within websites that allow companies to know when you've visited their site. Data from cookies can be linked to other sites and social media to *Retarget* prospects or for *Affiliate* marketing.
CRM	An acronym for "Customer Relationship Management." It's the communications arsenal you have in place to keep in contact with your customers. It can be email, *SMS*, or the like. But you're talking directly to your consumers.
Drive-By-Pitch	Think about an elevator pitch for your business, but distilled down to five-to-seven words. It should be simple, communicate your value proposition, distinct from other brands, and memorable.

E-commerce   It's what it sounds like. Buying, selling and advertising online. Whether it's *B2B* or *B2C*.

Endorsement Deal   When a celebrity, influencer, or otherwise popular entity agrees to promote your brand/product for some type of agreed compensation.

Equity   Equity means "owning a part of." Businesses can offer equity in stocks, inventory, or anything else that has value. Public companies list equity in publicly traded stocks, and many private companies offer equity to their employees as part of their benefits package.

First Mover Advantage   A fallacy in marketing. A first mover is the pioneer of a new product, service, or industry. The "first mover advantage" is the misconception that the first company in a new space will be the most successful one since they will grab a majority of the market share. Do you still use "Myspace"? Do you even know the name of the first mover in social media, "Friendster"? My guess is no.

FTC   Federal Trade Commission.

Gamification   Applying reward systems and traditionally video-game elements outside of the genre. Think about how games level up your character based on time spent or quests completed. There's a dopamine rush.

Growth-Stage Business

A business that has a *Minimum Viable Product* and has achieved some nascent success. They may be short on capital, but have the ability and hunger to scale. *Startups* are often no longer considered "startups" after they exit a major growth stage and have stability.

Gross Margin

More marketing math. It's your company's product cost subtracted from its total sales revenue, divided by that revenue. It's a percentage. How much did your product cost, how much did you make, and what's the percentage of the difference?

Impressions

A fancy marketing term for how likely someone is to see your advertisement where it's posted. Is it at the top of the page? Higher likelihood for impressions. Think back to the "Mad Men Era" of advertising: If your ad appeared right before the Table of Contents in a magazine, you're getting more eyeballs, and thus, more impressions.

Influencer Campaign

Using a social media influencer and/or celebrity to help promote your products. Can be useful if your interests align, but can be risky and ineffective if they don't.

Iterative

When you make subtle changes to your copy, design, or imagery in order to test the success of the different versions. You can iterate your outreach to determine which strategies resonate best with your audience. Not all mediums can be iterative since it's a one-time shot, e.g., podcasts or radio.

Incubator

Think *Silicon Valley* (the show). A business that provides resources to startups in order for them to develop.

K-Factor

Also known as the *Viral Coefficient*. It refers to how word-of-mouth awareness multiplies other marketing efforts. When something goes "viral," the marketing tends to take on a life of its own.

Lead Generation

Marketing jargon that means: getting more opportunities for more customers. Expanding your company's outreach to solidify more sales.

LTV

An acronym for "lifetime value." LTV considers how much revenue a customer will bring to your business throughout their continued loyalty, or purchasing "lifetime." Will they buy again? If so, how often and how much will they spend? Think one-time purchases v. subscriptions.

Masthead

For our use: Top-of-section headlines.

MVP Not your most valuable player, but potentially your most valuable metric. MVP is an acronym for "Minimum Viable Product." And there's a difference between Minimum Product and Minimum Viable Product. An MP is an early-stage product with just enough features to be tested and used by early adopters. An MP becomes an MVP, or viable, when it has an adequate consumer base to test its viability.

Native Advertising Advertising content that suits the design, language, and media of where it appears. The aim of this covert style is not to intrude on the user experience and dissuade them from engaging with the ad.

Open Rate Pretty simple: the percentage of your audience that opens your emails. *Clickthrough Rate* will then measure if they click on any links or content within the email.

Out-of-Home Advertising Out-of-Home Ads are what they sound like. Printed ads displayed for you to see, well, when you're outside. Billboards, posters, bus ads, and the like.

Portfolio Company A smaller company invested in and advised by a larger one. Many big-name companies generate capital by investing in smaller, portfolio companies for a piece of their pie. Raw capitalism at its core.

Purchase Cycle   Piggybacks on *Consideration Period*. Using a reasonable sample size, you can determine purchase cycles by averaging the duration of prospects' first engagements and their first respective purchases. In other words, the mathematical mean of your consideration period across all buyers.

Programmatic Marketing   A marketing tactic that uses machine learning and artificial intelligence to optimize your ad campaigns. Ideally, programmatic marketing can implement the most effective advertisements more quickly than a human, but the technology isn't advanced enough to consider complicated, non-logic-based values like customer profile, brand consistency, etc.

Remnant Space   TV ad space that hasn't been purchased, but still needs to be filled. You can think of it as "leftovers." Broadcast channels offer these ad spaces cheaper since they want all slots filled. The catch is you don't get to choose which programming your ad runs on.

Retargeting   You can retarget specific *Cohorts* of potential customers depending on if and when they've engaged with your content. It's a crucial piece of nurturing your audience.

ROAS
An acronym for "Return on Advertising Spend." Pretty simple: how much bang you get for your ad-budget buck. Be careful though. ROAS means nil if you don't look at it in context with *Consideration Period* and *LTV*.

ROI
An acronym for "Return on Investment." How much money you put in v. How much revenue generated. You can consider *ROAS* a measure of ROI, but ROI goes deeper—it's a measure of all budgets spent on a project. A square (ROI) is always a rectangle (*ROAS*) but a rectangle (*ROAS*) isn't always a square (ROI).

Sales Funnel
Your customers' journey from initial contact with the brand to purchasing a product or service. The goal is to expand your sales funnel, always. How can you extend your outreach? A sales funnel fails if its methods ignore any of the three principles.

Scale
An industry term for the period in which a company increases revenue faster than their costs. Cashflow wins the day, and the company can allocate more resources to expanding the team, sales funnel, ad expenses, etc.

SEO

An acronym for "Search Engine Optimization." Another piece of jargon, but its meaning is simple: how you attract more visitors to your site / social channels. There are loads of strategies and *B2B* companies who do it full time. But the most practical way to approach it is to make sure you have the right keywords in your content.

SMB

An acronym for "Small or Mid-Size Businesses."

SMS

More traditional term for a text message. But don't underestimate this tradition. SMS marketing blows email marketing out of the water by tenfold.

Startup

What it sounds like: a company in early stages of business. They may be fundraising, they may only be a few years old. The term has many applications.

Third-Party Validation

When an outside partner, press outlet, or other supporter talks positively about you and your business, building trust with new audiences and against naysayers.

Unit Economics

A more targeted measure of balancing revenues and costs. How much does *one product* or *one service* cost your company?

Value Proposition   A loaded term. Essentially, a concise statement of why your customers should hire you or purchase your product. What can you offer them, specifically? Why not hire the other guy next door?

VC   An acronym for "Venture Capitalist." VCs are individual investors or firms who tend to put money into startups or other riskier companies. The payoff can be high, so many smart VCs understand that loss is part of the game.

Viral Coefficient   See *K-Factor*.

Welcome Series   An initial, automated sequence of emails that thank new conversions and provide value for why they joined your email list in the first place. Be careful of offering too many discounts.

The Winback   Based upon your *Purchase Cycle*, a time-sensitive email that reaches out to customers or prospects who haven't engaged with your content over a specified period.

A free ebook edition is available with the purchase of this book.

To claim your free ebook edition:

1. Visit MorganJamesBOGO.com
2. Sign your name CLEARLY in the space
3. Complete the form and submit a photo of the entire copyright page
4. You or your friend can download the ebook to your preferred device

Print & Digital Together Forever.

Snap a photo

Free ebook

Read anywhere

CPSIA information can be obtained
at www.ICGtesting.com
Printed in the USA
LVHW091435130322
713343LV00006B/291

9 781631 957017